React.JS Question Bank

www.kansiris.org

by

Sireesh Kantamaneni

Dedication

I would like to say thanks to all my friends, to you and to readers or followers of my blog www.kansiris.org to encourage me to write this book which deserve to have theirs name on the cover as much as I do for all theirs support made this possible.

Sireesh Kantamaneni

Introduction

Writing a book has never been an easy task. It takes a great effort, patience and consistency with strong determination to complete it. Also, one should have a depth knowledge over the subject is going to write.

So, what where my qualification to write this book? My qualification and inspiration come from my enthusiasm for and the experience with the technology and from my analytic and initiative nature. Being software analyst, consultant and blogger, I have through knowledge and understandings of .NET technologies. My inspiration and knowledge has also come from many years of my working experience and research over it.

So, the next question is who this book is for? This book covers useful Interview Questions and Answers on .NET . This book is appropriate for novice as well as for senior level professionals who wants to strengthen their skills before appearing for an interview on ASP.NET MVC. This book is equally helpful to sharpen their programming skills and understanding .NET in a short time.

This book is not only the .NET interview book but it is more than that. This book helps you to get the depth knowledge of .NET with a simple and elegant way. This book is updated to latest version of .NET.

I hope you will enjoy this book and find it useful. At the same time I also encourage you to become a continue reader of the blog www.sirykt.blogspot.com and be the part of the discussion. But most importantly practice a lot and enjoy the technology. That's what it's all about.

To get the latest information on .NET, I encourage you to follow the official Microsoft ASP.NET community website at www.asp.net. I also encourage you to subscribe to my blog at www.kansiris.org that contains .NET, C#, ASP.NET MVC, EF, jQuery and many more tips, tricks and tutorials.

 Around 500 plus interview questions from live .NET interviews. Covers latest technology like Reporting services, Ajax, WCF, WPF and WWF. • During interviews other than main technology (.NET, JAVA etc.) companies expect other areas to be strong for example UML, Architecture, Database etc. Other sections are the most strong point of the book, which makes reader prepared for the unexpected questions. Full range of interview questions right from junior .NET developers to senior architects or project manager. Book covers important points like salary negotiations, resume making and general points to be remembered during interview. Recommended for .NET interviewers who are looking for what questions to be asked to get better and decent .NET professionals

Recommended for Fresher and students who want to have a feel of what .NET questions are asked in multinational companies. Developers who are looking for Quick reference and FAQ.

I am sure after reading this book reader will have extra confidence and a better approach for .NET interviews.

Changing job is one of the biggest events for any IT professional. When he starts the search he realizes that he needs much more than actual experience. Working on a project is one thing and cracking an interview is a different ball game, many may differ on this but that's my personal opinion.

When you work on a project you are doing a routine job and you tend to forget the basic fundamentals. For instance you are working on a highly technical project which uses remoting majorly in the project, it's very much possible that you can fail in simple ADO.NET questions because you are completely out of touch with it. We all know failing in simple ADO.NET questions will not even clear your first round. It does not mean you do not know the fundamentals; it's only that you need to revise the same. This book will give you bird eye view of what is needed in .NET interviews. It will help you in doing quick revision so that you can be ready for the interview in day or two. The best way to read this book is not from start to end rather just read the index and then go in details if needed.

This book covers the other aspect of .NET interviews by providing chapter like Architecture, UML, Reporting services, Ajax, SQL SERVER, Project Management, General Interview questions etc.

It's really good to see emails saying 'We got a job', just makes us feel better, please do write to us on siryblogz@gmail.com .I hope this book takes you to a better height and gives you extra confidence boost during interviews. Best of Luck and Happy Job-Hunting.............

All the best for your interview and happy programming!

About the author

Sireesh Kantamaneni

Works as Software Analyst at reputed MNC and has more than 7 years of hand over Microsoft .NET technologies. He is a .NET Consultant, founder and chief editor of www.kansiris.org .

A number of articles of him has become articles-of-the-day, selected in daily-community-spotlight, and listed in Recommended Resources for MVC section in The Official Microsoft ASP.NET Site. His blog www.kansiris.org is a well-known knowledge and support resource in the field of .NET technologies worldwide and is listed as a non-Microsoft resource in The Microsoft Official community Site.

He likes to share his working experience, research and knowledge through his well-known blogs.

He loves to work with web applications, Mobile apps and Mobile websites using Microsoft technology including C#, ASP.NET, ASP.NET MVC, SQL Server, WCF, WEB API, LINQ, Entity Framework, jQuery, jQuery UI, jQuery Mobile, Windows Azure, Angular, PhoneGap and many more web technologies.

He strives to be the best he can be. He always tries to gain more knowledge and skills in Microsoft technologies. He always keeps up with new technologies and learning new skills that allow him to provide better solutions to problems.

Table of Contents

ReactJS

Core React

Question: What is React?

React is an open-source frontend JavaScript library which is used for building user interfaces especially for single page applications. It is used for handling view layer for web and mobile apps. React was created by Jordan Walke, a software engineer working for Facebook. React was first deployed on Facebook's News Feed in 2011 and on Instagram in 2012.

Question: What are the major features of React?

The major features of React are:

It uses VirtualDOM instead RealDOM considering that RealDOM manipulations are expensive.

Supports server-side rendering.

Follows Unidirectional* data flow or data binding.

Uses reusable/composable UI components to develop the view.

Question: What is JSX?

JSX is a XML-like syntax extension to ECMAScript (the acronym stands for JavaScript XML). Basically it just provides syntactic sugar for the React.createElement() function, giving us expressiveness of JavaScript along with HTML like template syntax.

In the example below text inside <h1> tag return as JavaScript function to the render function.

```
class App extends React.Component {

 render() {   return(    <div>     <h1>{'Welcome to React world!'}</h1></div>   )}}
```

Question: What is the difference between Element and Component?

An Element is a plain object describing what you want to appear on the screen in terms of the DOM nodes or other components. Elements can contain other Elements in their props. Creating a React element is cheap. Once an element is created, it is never mutated.

The object representation of React Element would be as follows:

```
const element = React.createElement(

 'div',

 {id: 'login-btn'},

 'Login')
```

The above React.createElement() function returns an object:

```
{ type: 'div',

 props: {   children: 'Login',   id: 'login-btn'  }}
```

And finally it renders to the DOM using ReactDOM.render():

```
<div id='login-btn'>Login</div>
```

Whereas a component can be declared in several different ways. It can be a class with a render() method. Alternatively, in simple cases, it can be defined as a function. In either case, it takes props as an input, and returns an JSX tree as the output:

```
const Button = ({ onLogin }) =>

 <div id={'login-btn'} onClick={onLogin} />
```

Then JSX gets transpiled to React.createElement() function tree:

```
const Button = ({ onLogin }) => React.createElement(

 'div',  { id: 'login-btn', onClick: onLogin },

 'Login')
```

Question: How to create components in React?

There are two possible ways to create a component.

Function Components: This is the simplest way to create a component. Those are pure JavaScript functions that accept props object as first parameter and return React elements:

```
function Greeting({ message }) {  return <h1>{`Hello, ${message}`}</h1>  }
```

Class Components: You can also use ES6 class to define a component. The above function component can be written as:

```
class Greeting extends React.Component {

 render() {   return <h1>{`Hello, ${this.props.message}`}</h1>  }}
```

Question: When to use a Class Component over a Function Component?

If the component needs state or lifecycle methods then use class component otherwise use function component.

Question: What are Pure Components?

React.PureComponent is exactly the same as React.Component except that it handles the shouldComponentUpdate() method for you. When props or state changes, PureComponent will do a shallow comparison on both props and state. Component on the other hand won't compare current props and state to next out of the box. Thus, the component will re-render by default whenever shouldComponentUpdate is called.

Question: What is state in React?

State of a component is an object that holds some information that may change over the lifetime of the component. We should always try to make our state as simple as possible and minimize the number of stateful components. Let's create an user component with message state,

```
class User extends React.Component {

 constructor(props) {   super(props)
```

this.state = {   message: 'Welcome to React world'   } }

render() {   return (<div>   <h1>{this.state.message}</h1>   </div>   ) } }

state

State is similar to props, but it is private and fully controlled by the component. i.e, It is not accessible to any component other than the one that owns and sets it.

Question: What are props in React?

Props are inputs to components. They are single values or objects containing a set of values that are passed to components on creation using a naming convention similar to HTML-tag attributes. They are data passed down from a parent component to a child component.

The primary purpose of props in React is to provide following component functionality:

Pass custom data to your component.

Trigger state changes.

Use via this.props.reactProp inside component's render() method.

For example, let us create an element with reactProp property:

<Element reactProp={'1'} />

This reactProp (or whatever you came up with) name then becomes a property attached to React's native props object which originally already exists on all components created using React library.

props.reactProp

Question: What is the difference between state and props?

Both props and state are plain JavaScript objects. While both of them hold information that influences the output of render, they are different in their functionality with respect to component. Props get passed to the component similar to function parameters whereas state is managed within the component similar to variables declared within a function.

Question: Why should we not update the state directly?

If you try to update state directly then it won't re-render the component.

//Wrong

this.state.message = 'Hello world'

Instead use setState() method. It schedules an update to a component's state object. When state changes, the component responds by re-rendering.

//Correct

this.setState({ message: 'Hello World' })

Note: You can directly assign to the state object either in constructor or using latest javascript's class field declaration syntax.

Question: What is the purpose of callback function as an argument of setState()?

The callback function is invoked when setState finished and the component gets rendered. Since setState() is asynchronous the callback function is used for any post action.

Note: It is recommended to use lifecycle method rather than this callback function.
setState({ name: 'John' }, () => console.log('The name has updated and component re-rendered'))

Question: What is the difference between HTML and React event handling?

In HTML, the event name should be in lowercase:

<button onclick='activateLasers()'>

Whereas in React it follows camelCase convention:

<button onClick={activateLasers}>

In HTML, you can return false to prevent default behavior:

<a href='#' onclick='console.log("The link was clicked."); return false;' />

Whereas in React you must call preventDefault() explicitly:

function handleClick(event) {   event.preventDefault()   console.log('The link was clicked.')}

Question: How to bind methods or event handlers in JSX callbacks?

There are 3 possible ways to achieve this:

Binding in Constructor: In JavaScript classes, the methods are not bound by default. The same thing applies for React event handlers defined as class methods. Normally we bind them in constructor.

class Component extends React.Componenet {

  constructor(props) {   super(props)   this.handleClick = this.handleClick.bind(this)   }

  handleClick() {

```
// ...

}}
```

Public class fields syntax: If you don't like to use bind approach then public class fields syntax can be used to correctly bind callbacks.

```
handleClick = () => { console.log('this is:', this)}

<button onClick={this.handleClick}> {'Click me'} </button>
```

Arrow functions in callbacks: You can use arrow functions directly in the callbacks.

```
<button onClick={(event) => this.handleClick(event)}> {'Click me'}</button>
```

Note: If the callback is passed as prop to child components, those components might do an extra re-rendering. In those cases, it is preferred to go with .bind() or public class fields syntax approach considering performance.

Question: How to pass a parameter to an event handler or callback?

You can use an arrow function to wrap around an event handler and pass parameters:

```
<button onClick={() => this.handleClick(id)} />
```

This is an equivalent to calling .bind:

```
<button onClick={this.handleClick.bind(this, id)} />
```

Question: What are synthetic events in React?

SyntheticEvent is a cross-browser wrapper around the browser's native event. It's API is same as the browser's native event, including stopPropagation() and preventDefault(), except the events work identically across all browsers.

Question: What is inline conditional expressions?

You can use either if statements or ternary expressions which are available from JS to conditionally render expressions. Apart from these approaches, you can also embed any expressions in JSX by wrapping them in curly braces and then followed by JS logical operator &&.

```
<h1>Hello!</h1>

{ messages.length > 0 && !isLogin? <h2>  You have {messages.length} unread messages.   </h2>
:   <h2>      You don't have unread messages.   </h2>}
```

Question: What are "key" props and what is the benefit of using them in arrays of elements?

A key is a special string attribute you should include when creating arrays of elements. Keys help React identify which items have changed, are added, or are removed.

Most often we use IDs from our data as keys:

const todoItems = todos.map((todo) => <li key={todo.id}> {todo.text} </li>)

When you don't have stable IDs for rendered items, you may use the item index as a key as a last resort:

const todoItems = todos.map((todo, index) => <li key={index}> {todo.text} </li>)

Note:
Using indexes for keys is not recommended if the order of items may change. This can negatively impact performance and may cause issues with component state.

If you extract list item as separate component then apply keys on list component instead of li tag.

There will be a warning message in the console if the key prop is not present on list items.

Question: What is the use of refs?

The ref is used to return a reference to the element. They should be avoided in most cases, however, they can be useful when you need a direct access to the DOM element or an instance of a component.

Question: How to create refs?

There are two approachesThis is a recently added approach. Refs are created using React.createRef() method and attached to React elements via the ref attribute. In order to use refs throughout the component, just assign the ref to the instance property within constructor.

class MyComponent extends React.Component {

  constructor(props) {   super(props)

   this.myRef = React.createRef() }

  render() {   return   }}

You can also use ref callbacks approach regardless of React version. For example, the search bar component's input element accessed as follows,

class SearchBar extends Component {

  constructor(props) {

    super(props);   this.txtSearch = null;   this.state = { term: '' };   this.setInputSearchRef = e => {

```
      this.txtSearch = e;    } }

  onInputChange(event) {    this.setState({ term: this.txtSearch.value });  }

  render() {    return (        <input  value={this.state.term}
onChange={this.onInputChange.bind(this)}

        ref={this.setInputSearchRef} />    );  }}
```

You can also use refs in function components using closures. Note: You can also use inline ref callbacks even though it is not a recommended approach

Question: What are forward refs?

Ref forwarding is a feature that lets some components take a ref they receive, and pass it further down to a child.

```
const ButtonElement = React.forwardRef((props, ref) => (

  <button ref={ref} className="CustomButton">   {props.children}  </button>));

// Create ref to the DOM button:

const ref = React.createRef();

<ButtonElement ref={ref}>{'Forward Ref'}</ButtonElement>
```

Question: Which is preferred option with in callback refs and findDOMNode()?

It is preferred to use callback refs over findDOMNode() API. Because findDOMNode() prevents certain improvements in React in the future.

The legacy approach of using findDOMNode:

```
class MyComponent extends Component {

  componentDidMount() {   findDOMNode(this).scrollIntoView()  }

  render() {   return <div /> }}
```

The recommended approach is:

```
class MyComponent extends Component {

  componentDidMount() {    this.node.scrollIntoView()  }

  render() {   return <div ref={node => this.node = node} />  }}
```

Question: Why are String Refs legacy?

If you worked with React before, you might be familiar with an older API where the ref attribute is a string, like ref={'textInput'}, and the DOM node is accessed as this.refs.textInput. We advise against it because string refs have below issues, and are considered legacy. String refs were removed in React v16.

They force React to keep track of currently executing component. This is problematic because it makes react module stateful, and thus causes weird errors when react module is duplicated in the bundle.

They are not composable — if a library puts a ref on the passed child, the user can't put another ref on it. Callback refs are perfectly composable.

They don't work with static analysis like Flow. Flow can't guess the magic that framework does to make the string ref appear on this.refs, as well as its type (which could be different). Callback refs are friendlier to static analysis.

It doesn't work as most people would expect with the "render callback" pattern (e.g.)

```
class MyComponent extends Component {

  renderRow = (index) => {

    // This won't work. Ref will get attached to DataTable rather than MyComponent:

    return <input ref={'input-' + index} />;

    // This would work though! Callback refs are awesome.

    return <input ref={input => this['input-' + index] = input} />;  }

  render() {    return <DataTable data={this.props.data} renderRow={thls.renderRow} />  }}
```

Question: What is Virtual DOM?

The Virtual DOM (VDOM) is an in-memory representation of Real DOM. The representation of a UI is kept in memory and synced with the "real" DOM. It's a step that happens between the render function being called and the displaying of elements on the screen. This entire process is called reconciliation.

Question: How Virtual DOM works?

The Virtual DOM works in three simple steps.

Whenever any underlying data changes, the entire UI is re-rendered in Virtual DOM representation.
Vdom

Then the difference between the previous DOM representation and the new one is calculated. vdom2

Once the calculations are done, the real DOM will be updated with only the things that have actually changed. vdom3

Question: What is the difference between Shadow DOM and Virtual DOM?

The Shadow DOM is a browser technology designed primarily for scoping variables and CSS in web components. The Virtual DOM is a concept implemented by libraries in JavaScript on top of browser APIs.

Question: What is React Fiber?

Fiber is the new reconciliation engine or reimplementation of core algorithm in React v16. The goal of React Fiber is to increase its suitability for areas like animation, layout, gestures, ability to pause, abort, or reuse work and assign priority to different types of updates; and new concurrency primitives.

Question: What is the main goal of React Fiber?

The goal of React Fiber is to increase its suitability for areas like animation, layout, and gestures. Its headline feature is incremental rendering: the ability to split rendering work into chunks and spread it out over multiple frames.

Question: What are controlled components?

A component that controls the input elements within the forms on subsequent user input is called Controlled Component, i.e, every state mutation will have an associated handler function.

For example, to write all the names in uppercase letters, we use handleChange as below,

handleChange(event) { this.setState({value: event.target.value.toUpperCase()}})}

Question: What are uncontrolled components?

The Uncontrolled Components are the ones that store their own state internally, and you query the DOM using a ref to find its current value when you need it. This is a bit more like traditional HTML.

In the below UserProfile component, the name input is accessed using ref.

class UserProfile extends React.Component {

 constructor(props) {   super(props)

  this.handleSubmit = this.handleSubmit.bind(this)

  this.input = React.createRef() }

 handleSubmit(event) {   alert('A name was submitted: ' + this.input.current.value)

```
event.preventDefault() }

render() {   return (     <form onSubmit={this.handleSubmit}>

    <label>      {'Name:'}      <input type="text" ref={this.input} />      </label>

    <input type="submit" value="Submit" />      </form>   ); }}
```

In most cases, it's recommend to use controlled components to implement forms.

Question: What is the difference between createElement and cloneElement?

JSX elements will be transpiled to React.createElement() functions to create React elements which are going to be used for the object representation of UI. Whereas cloneElement is used to clone an element and pass it new props.

Question: What is Lifting State Up in React?

When several components need to share the same changing data then it is recommended to lift the shared state up to their closest common ancestor. That means if two child components share the same data from its parent, then move the state to parent instead of maintaining local state in both of the child components.

Question: What are the different phases of component lifecycle?

There are four different phases of component lifecycle.

Initialization: In this phase component prepares setting up the initial state and default props.

Mounting: The component is ready to mount in the browser DOM. This phase covers componentWillMount() and componentDidMount() lifecycle methods.

Updating: In this phase, the component get updated in two ways, sending the new props and updating the state. This phase covers shouldComponentUpdate(), componentWillUpdate() and componentDidUpdate() lifecycle methods.

Unmounting: In this last phase, the component is not needed and get unmounted from the browser DOM. This phase includes componentWillUnmount() lifecycle method. phases

Question: What are the lifecycle methods of React?

componentWillMount: Executed before rendering and is used for App level configuration in your root component.

componentDidMount: Executed after first rendering and here all AJAX requests, DOM or state updates, and set up event listeners should occur.

componentWillReceiveProps: Executed when particular prop updates to trigger state transitions.

shouldComponentUpdate: Determines if the component will be updated or not. By default it returns true. If you are sure that the component doesn't need to render after state or props are updated, you can return false value. It is a great place to improve performance as it allows you to prevent a re-render if component receives new prop.

componentWillUpdate: Executed before re-rendering the component when there are props & state changes confirmed by shouldComponentUpdate() which returns true.

componentDidUpdate: Mostly it is used to update the DOM in response to prop or state changes.

componentWillUnmount: It will be used to cancel any outgoing network requests, or remove all event listeners associated with the component.

Question: What are Higher-Order Components?

A higher-order component (HOC) is a function that takes a component and returns a new component. Basically, it's a pattern that is derived from React's compositional nature.

We call them pure components because they can accept any dynamically provided child component but they won't modify or copy any behavior from their input components.

const EnhancedComponent = higherOrderComponent(WrappedComponent)

HOC can be used for many use cases:

Code reuse, logic and bootstrap abstraction.

Render hijacking.

State abstraction and manipulation.

Props manipulation.

Question: How to create props proxy for HOC component?

You can add/edit props passed to the component using props proxy pattern like this:

```
function HOC(WrappedComponent) {

  return class Test extends Component {

    render() {    const newProps = {    title: 'New Header',

      footer: false,    showFeatureX: false,    showFeatureY: true    }

      return <WrappedComponent {...this.props} {...newProps} />   } }}
```

Question: What is context?

Context provides a way to pass data through the component tree without having to pass props down manually at every level. For example, authenticated user, locale preference, UI theme need to be accessed in the application by many components.

const {Provider, Consumer} = React.createContext(defaultValue)

Question: What is children prop?

Children is a prop (this.prop.children) that allow you to pass components as data to other components, just like any other prop you use. Component tree put between component's opening and closing tag will be passed to that component as children prop.

There are a number of methods available in the React API to work with this prop. These include React.Children.map, React.Children.forEach, React.Children.count, React.Children.only, React.Children.toArray. A simple usage of children prop looks as below,

const MyDiv = React.createClass({

  render: function() {   return <div>{this.props.children}</div> }})

ReactDOM.render(<MyDiv> <span>{'Hello'}</span>   <span>{'World'}</span> </MyDiv>, node)

Question: How to write comments in React?

The comments in React/JSX are similar to JavaScript Multiline comments but are wrapped in curly braces.

Single-line comments:

<div> {/* Single-line comments(In vanilla JavaScript, the single-line comments are represented by double slash(//)) */} {`Welcome ${user}, let's play React`}</div>

Multi-line comments:

<div> {/* Multi-line comments for more than   one line */}

 {`Welcome ${user}, let's play React`}</div>

Question: What is the purpose of using super constructor with props argument?

A child class constructor cannot make use of this reference until super() method has been called. The same applies for ES6 sub-classes as well. The main reason of passing props parameter to super() call is to access this.props in your child constructors.

Passing props:

```
class MyComponent extends React.Component {

  constructor(props) {   super(props)

    console.log(this.props) // prints { name: 'John', age: 42 }  }}
```

Not passing props:

```
class MyComponent extends React.Component {

  constructor(props) {   super()

    console.log(this.props) // prints undefined

    // but props parameter is still available

    console.log(props) // prints { name: 'John', age: 42 }}

  render() {   // no difference outside constructor

    console.log(this.props) // prints { name: 'John', age: 42 }}}
```

The above code snippets reveals that this.props is different only within the constructor. It would be the same outside the constructor.

Question: What is reconciliation?

When a component's props or state change, React decides whether an actual DOM update is necessary by comparing the newly returned element with the previously rendered one. When they are not equal, React will update the DOM. This process is called reconciliation.

Question: How to set state with a dynamic key name?

If you are using ES6 or the Babel transpiler to transform your JSX code then you can accomplish this with computed property names.

```
handleInputChange(event) {  this.setState({ [event.target.id]: event.target.value })}
```

What would be the common mistake of function being called every time the component renders?

You need to make sure that function is not being called while passing the function as a parameter.

```
render() {

  // Wrong: handleClick is called instead of passed as a reference!

  return <button onClick={this.handleClick()}>{'Click Me'}</button>}
```

Instead, pass the function itself without parenthesis:

render() { // Correct: handleClick is passed as a reference!

  return <button onClick={this.handleClick}>{'Click Me'}</button>}

Question: Why is it necessary to capitalize component names?

It is necessary because components are not DOM elements, they are constructors. Also, in JSX lowercase tag names are referring to HTML elements, not components.

Question: Why React uses className over class attribute?

class is a keyword in JavaSript, and JSX is an extension of JavaScript. That's the principal reason why React uses className instead of class. Pass a string as the className prop.

render() { return <span className={'menu navigation-menu'}>{'Menu'}}

Question: What are fragments?

It's common pattern in React which is used for a component to return multiple elements. Fragments let you group a list of children without adding extra nodes to the DOM.

render() { return (<React.Fragment> <ChildA />   <ChildB /> <ChildC />   </React.Fragment>)}

There is also a shorter syntax, but it's not supported in many tools:

render() { return (<><ChildA /> <ChildB /> <ChildC /> </>)}

Question: Why fragments are better than container divs?

Fragments are a bit faster and use less memory by not creating an extra DOM node. This only has a real benefit on very large and deep trees.

Some CSS mechanisms like Flexbox and CSS Grid have a special parent-child relationships, and adding divs in the middle makes it hard to keep the desired layout.

The DOM Inspector is less cluttered.

Question: What are portals in React?

Portal is a recommended way to render children into a DOM node that exists outside the DOM hierarchy of the parent component.

ReactDOM.createPortal(child, container)

The first argument is any render-able React child, such as an element, string, or fragment. The second argument is a DOM element.

Question: What are stateless components?

If the behaviour is independent of its state then it can be a stateless component. You can use either a function or a class for creating stateless components. But unless you need to use a lifecycle hook in your components, you should go for function components. There are a lot of benefits if you decide to use function components here; they are easy to write, understand, and test, a little faster, and you can avoid the this keyword altogether.

Question: What are stateful components?

If the behaviour of a component is dependent on the state of the component then it can be termed as stateful component. These stateful components are always class components and have a state that gets initialized in the constructor.

```
class App extends Component {

  constructor(props) {   super(props)

   this.state = { count: 0 }  }

  render() {   ... }}
```

Question: How to apply validation on props in React?

When the application is running in development mode, React will automatically check all props that we set on components to make sure they have correct type. If the type is incorrect, React will generate warning messages in the console. It's disabled in production mode due performance impact. The mandatory props are defined with isRequired.

The set of predefined prop types:

PropTypes.number

PropTypes.string

PropTypes.array

PropTypes.object

PropTypes.func

PropTypes.node

PropTypes.element

PropTypes.bool

PropTypes.symbol

PropTypes.any

We can define propTypes for User component as below:

import React from 'react'

import PropTypes from 'prop-types'

class User extends React.Component {

  static propTypes = {   name: PropTypes.string.isRequired,   age: PropTypes.number.isRequired }

  render() {   return (<>   <h1>{`Welcome, ${this.props.name}`}</h1>

    <h2>{`Age, ${this.props.age}`}</h2>   </>   ) }}

Note: In React v15.5 PropTypes were moved from React.PropTypes to prop-types library.

Question: What are the advantages of React?

Increases the application's performance with Virtual DOM.

JSX makes code easy to read and write.

It renders both on client and server side (SSR).

Easy to integrate with frameworks (Angular, Backbone) since it is only a view library.

Easy to write unit and integration tests with tools such as Jest.

Question: What are the limitations of React?

React is just a view library, not a full framework.

There is a learning curve for beginners who are new to web development.

Integrating React into a traditional MVC framework requires some additional configuration.

The code complexity increases with inline templating and JSX.

Too many smaller components leading to over engineering or boilerplate.

Question: What are error boundaries in React v16?

Error boundaries are components that catch JavaScript errors anywhere in their child component tree, log those errors, and display a fallback UI instead of the component tree that crashed.

A class component becomes an error boundary if it defines a new lifecycle method called componentDidCatch(error, info) or static getDerivedStateFromError() :

```
class ErrorBoundary extends React.Component {

  constructor(props) {   super(props)

   this.state = { hasError: false }  }

  componentDidCatch(error, info) {   // You can also log the error to an error reporting service

   logErrorToMyService(error, info)  }

  static getDerivedStateFromError(error) {

    // Update state so the next render will show the fallback UI.

    return { hasError: true };  }

  render() {    if (this.state.hasError) {     // You can render any custom fallback UI

      return <h1>{'Something went wrong.'}</h1>   }   return this.props.children  }}
```

After that use it as a regular component:<ErrorBoundary> <MyWidget /></ErrorBoundary>

Question: How error boundaries handled in React v15?

React v15 provided very basic support for error boundaries using unstable_handleError method. It has been renamed to componentDidCatch in React v16.

Question: What are the recommended ways for static type checking?

Normally we use PropTypes library (React.PropTypes moved to a prop-types package since React v15.5) for type checking in the React applications. For large code bases, it is recommended to use static type checkers such as Flow or TypeScript, that perform type checking at compile time and provide auto-completion features.

Question: What is the use of react-dom package?

The react-dom package provides DOM-specific methods that can be used at the top level of your app. Most of the components are not required to use this module. Some of the methods of this package are:

render()

hydrate()

unmountComponentAtNode()

findDOMNode()

createPortal()

Question: What is the purpose of render method of react-dom?

This method is used to render a React element into the DOM in the supplied container and return a reference to the component. If the React element was previously rendered into container, it will perform an update on it and only mutate the DOM as necessary to reflect the latest changes.

ReactDOM.render(element, container[, callback])

If the optional callback is provided, it will be executed after the component is rendered or updated.

Question: What is ReactDOMServer?

The ReactDOMServer object enables you to render components to static markup (typically used on node server). This object is mainly used for server-side rendering (SSR). The following methods can be used in both the server and browser environments:

renderToString()

renderToStaticMarkup()

For example, you generally run a Node-based web server like Express, Hapi, or Koa, and you call renderToString to render your root component to a string, which you then send as response.

```
// using Express
import { renderToString } from 'react-dom/server'
import MyPage from './MyPage'
app.get('/', (req, res) => {
  res.write('<!DOCTYPE html><html><head><title>My Page</title></head><body>')
  res.write('<div id="content">')
  res.write(renderToString(<MyPage/>))
  res.write('</div></body></html>')
  res.end()
})
```

Question: How to use innerHTML in React?

The dangerouslySetInnerHTML attribute is React's replacement for using innerHTML in the browser DOM. Just like innerHTML, it is risky to use this attribute considering cross-site scripting (XSS) attacks. You just need to pass a __html object as key and HTML text as value.

In this example MyComponent uses dangerouslySetInnerHTML attribute for setting HTML markup:

```
function createMarkup() {

  return { __html: 'First &middot; Second' }}

function MyComponent() {  return <div dangerouslySetInnerHTML={createMarkup()} />}
```

Question: How to use styles in React?

The style attribute accepts a JavaScript object with camelCased properties rather than a CSS string. This is consistent with the DOM style JavaScript property, is more efficient, and prevents XSS security holes.

```
const divStyle = {  color: 'blue',  backgroundImage: 'url(' + imgUrl + ')'};

function HelloWorldComponent() {  return <div style={divStyle}>Hello World!</div>}
```

Style keys are camelCased in order to be consistent with accessing the properties on DOM nodes in JavaScript (e.g. node.style.backgroundImage).

Question: How events are different in React?

Handling events in React elements has some syntactic differences:

React event handlers are named using camelCase, rather than lowercase.

With JSX you pass a function as the event handler, rather than a string.

Question: What will happen if you use setState() in constructor?

When you use setState(), then apart from assigning to the object state React also re-renders the component and all its children. You would get error like this: Can only update a mounted or mounting component. So we need to use this.state to initialize variables inside constructor.

Question: What is the impact of indexes as keys?

Keys should be stable, predictable, and unique so that React can keep track of elements.

In the below code snippet each element's key will be based on ordering, rather than tied to the data that is being represented. This limits the optimizations that React can do.

```
{todos.map((todo, index) =>  <Todo    {...todo}   key={index}  /> )}
```

If you use element data for unique key, assuming todo.id is unique to this list and stable, React would be able to reorder elements without needing to reevaluate them as much.

```
{todos.map((todo) =>  <Todo {...todo}   key={todo.id} /> )}
```

Question: Is it good to use setState() in componentWillMount() method?

It is recommended to avoid async initialization in componentWillMount() lifecycle method. componentWillMount() is invoked immediately before mounting occurs. It is called before render(), therefore setting state in this method will not trigger a re-render. Avoid introducing any side-effects or subscriptions in this method. We need to make sure async calls for component initialization happened in componentDidMount() instead of componentWillMount().

```
componentDidMount() {

  axios.get(`api/todos`)

   .then((result) => {     this.setState({     messages: [...result.data]     })   }) }
```

Question: What will happen if you use props in initial state?

If the props on the component are changed without the component being refreshed, the new prop value will never be displayed because the constructor function will never update the current state of the component. The initialization of state from props only runs when the component is first created.

The below component won't display the updated input value:

```
class MyComponent extends React.Component {

  constructor(props) {   super(props)

    this.state = {    records: [],    inputValue: this.props.inputValue   };  }

  render() {    return <div>{this.state.inputValue}</div>  }}
```

Using props inside render method will update the value:

```
class MyComponent extends React.Component {

  constructor(props) {   super(props)

    this.state = {    record: []    }  }

  render() {    return <div>{this.props.inputValue}</div>  }}
```

Question: How do you conditionally render components?

In some cases you want to render different components depending on some state. JSX does not render false or undefined, so you can use conditional short-circuiting to render a given part of your component only if a certain condition is true.

```
const MyComponent = ({ name, address }) => ( <div> <h2>{name}</h2>   {address &&
<p>{address}</p>   } </div> )
```

If you need an if-else condition then use ternary operator.

```
const MyComponent = ({ name, address }) => ( <div> <h2>{name}</h2>   {address

  ? <p>{address}</p>    : <p>{'Address is not available'}</p>   } </div> )
```

Why we need to be careful when spreading props on DOM elements?

When we spread props we run into the risk of adding unknown HTML attributes, which is a bad practice. Instead we can use prop destructuring with ...rest operator, so it will add only required props. For example,

```
const ComponentA = () =>  <ComponentB isDisplay={true} className={'componentStyle'} />

const ComponentB = ({ isDisplay, ...domProps }) =>  <div {...domProps}>{'ComponentB'}</div>
```

How you use decorators in React?

You can decorate your class components, which is the same as passing the component into a function. Decorators are flexible and readable way of modifying component functionality.

```
@setTitle('Profile')

class Profile extends React.Component {

  //....

}

/*

  title is a string that will be set as a document title

  WrappedComponent is what our decorator will receive when

  put directly above a component class as seen in the example above

*/

const setTitle = (title) => (WrappedComponent) => {

  return class extends React.Component {
```

```
componentDidMount() {    document.title = title}

render() {    return <WrappedComponent {...this.props} /> } } }
```

Note: Decorators are a feature that didn't make it into ES7, but are currently a stage 2 proposal.

Question: How do you memoize a component?

There are memoize libraries available which can be used on function components. For example moize library can memoize the component in another component.

import moize from 'moize'

import Component from './components/Component' // this module exports a non-memoized component

const MemoizedFoo = moize.react(Component)

const Consumer = () => {

  <div>   {'I will memoize the following entry:'} <MemoizedFoo/> </div> }

Question: How you implement Server Side Rendering or SSR?

React is already equipped to handle rendering on Node servers. A special version of the DOM renderer is available, which follows the same pattern as on the client side.

import ReactDOMServer from 'react-dom/server'

import App from './App'

ReactDOMServer.renderToString(<App />)

This method will output the regular HTML as a string, which can be then placed inside a page body as part of the server response. On the client side, React detects the pre-rendered content and seamlessly picks up where it left off.

Question: How to enable production mode in React?

You should use Webpack's DefinePlugin method to set NODE_ENV to production, by which it strip out things like propType validation and extra warnings. Apart from this, if you minify the code, for example, Uglify's dead-code elimination to strip out development only code and comments, it will drastically reduce the size of your bundle.

Question: What is CRA and its benefits?

The create-react-app CLI tool allows you to quickly create & run React applications with no configuration step.

Let's create Todo App using CRA:

Installation

$ npm install -g create-react-app

Create new project

$ create-react-app todo-app

$ cd todo-app

Build, test and run

$ npm run build

$ npm run test

$ npm start

It includes everything we need to build a React app:

React, JSX, ES6, and Flow syntax support.

Language extras beyond ES6 like the object spread operator.

Autoprefixed CSS, so you don't need -webkit- or other prefixes.

A fast interactive unit test runner with built-in support for coverage reporting.

A live development server that warns about common mistakes.

A build script to bundle JS, CSS, and images for production, with hashes and sourcemaps.

Question: What is the lifecycle methods order in mounting?

The lifecycle methods are called in the following order when an instance of a component is being created and inserted into the DOM.

constructor()

static getDerivedStateFromProps()

render()

componentDidMount()

Question: What are the lifecycle methods going to be deprecated in React v16?

The following lifecycle methods going to be unsafe coding practices and will be more problematic with async rendering.

componentWillMount()

componentWillReceiveProps()

componentWillUpdate()

Starting with React v16.3 these methods are aliased with UNSAFE_ prefix, and the unprefixed version will be removed in React v17.

Question: What is the purpose of getDerivedStateFromProps() lifecycle method?

The new static getDerivedStateFromProps() lifecycle method is invoked after a component is instantiated as well as before it is re-rendered. It can return an object to update state, or null to indicate that the new props do not require any state updates.

class MyComponent extends React.Component {

  static getDerivedStateFromProps(props, state) {

    // ...

  }}

This lifecycle method along with componentDidUpdate() covers all the use cases of componentWillReceiveProps().

Question:What is the purpose of getSnapshotBeforeUpdate() lifecycle method?

The new getSnapshotBeforeUpdate() lifecycle method is called right before DOM updates. The return value from this method will be passed as the third parameter to componentDidUpdate().

class MyComponent extends React.Component {

  getSnapshotBeforeUpdate(prevProps, prevState) {

    // ...

  }}

This lifecycle method along with componentDidUpdate() covers all the use cases of componentWillUpdate().

Question: What is the difference between createElement() and cloneElement() methods?

In JSX the React element is transpiled to React.createElement() which represents an UI element. Whereas React.cloneElement() is used in order to clone an element and pass it new props.

Question: What is the recommended way for naming components?

It is recommended to name the component by reference instead of using displayName.

Using displayName for naming component:

export default React.createClass({   displayName: 'TodoApp',

 // ...

})

The recommended approach:

export default class TodoApp extends React.Component {

 // ...

}

Question: What is the recommended ordering of methods in component class?

Recommended ordering of methods from mounting to render stage:

static methods

constructor()

getChildContext()

componentWillMount()

componentDidMount()

componentWillReceiveProps()

shouldComponentUpdate()

componentWillUpdate()

componentDidUpdate()

componentWillUnmount()

click handlers or event handlers like onClickSubmit() or onChangeDescription()

getter methods for render like getSelectReason() or getFooterContent()

optional render methods like renderNavigation() or renderProfilePicture()

render()

Question: What is a switching component?

A switching component is a component that renders one of many components. We need to use object to map prop values to components.

For example, a switching component to display different pages based on page prop:

```
import HomePage from './HomePage'

import AboutPage from './AboutPage'

import ServicesPage from './ServicesPage'

import ContactPage from './ContactPage'

const PAGES = {

  home: HomePage,

  about: AboutPage,

  services: ServicesPage,

  contact: ContactPage

}

const Page = (props) => {  const Handler = PAGES[props.page] || ContactPage

  return <Handler {...props} />  }

// The keys of the PAGES object can be used in the prop types to catch dev-time errors.

Page.propTypes = { page: PropTypes.oneOf(Object.keys(PAGES)).isRequired  }
```

Question: Why we need to pass a function to setState()?

The reason behind for this is that setState() is an asynchronous operation. React batches state changes for performance reasons, so the state may not change immediately after setState() is called. That means you should not rely on the current state when calling setState()since you can't be sure what that state will be. The solution is topass a function to setState(), with the previous state as an argument. By doing this you can avoid issues with the user getting the old state value on access due to the asynchronous nature of setState().

Let's say the initial count value is zero. After three consecutive increment operations, the value is going to be incremented only by one.

```
// assuming this.state.count === 0

this.setState({ count: this.state.count + 1 })

this.setState({ count: this.state.count + 1 })

this.setState({ count: this.state.count + 1 })

// this.state.count === 1, not 3
```

If we pass a function to setState(), the count gets incremented correctly.

```
this.setState((prevState, props) => ({ count: prevState.count + props.increment }))

// this.state.count === 3 as expected
```

Question: What is strict mode in React?

React.StrictMode is an useful component for highlighting potential problems in an application. Just like <Fragment>, <StrictMode> does not render any extra DOM elements. It activates additional checks and warnings for its descendants. These checks apply for development mode only.

```
import React from 'react'

function ExampleApplication() {

  return (

    <div>    <Header /> <React.StrictMode>

      <div>       <ComponentOne />        <ComponentTwo />       </div>

    </React.StrictMode>    <Footer />   </div>  ) }
```

In the example above, the strict mode checks apply to <ComponentOne> and <ComponentTwo> components only.

Question: What are React Mixins?

Mixins are a way to totally separate components to have a common functionality. Mixins are should not be used and can be replaced with higher-order components or decorators.

One of the most commonly used mixins is PureRenderMixin. You might be using it in some components to prevent unnecessary re-renders when the props and state are shallowly equal to the previous props and state:

```
const PureRenderMixin = require('react-addons-pure-render-mixin')

const Button = React.createClass({

  mixins: [PureRenderMixin],

  // ...

})
```

Why is isMounted() an anti-pattern and what is the proper solution?

The primary use case for isMounted() is to avoid calling setState() after a component has been unmounted, because it will emit a warning.

```
if (this.isMounted()) {   this.setState({...}) }
```

Checking isMounted() before calling setState() does eliminate the warning, but it also defeats the purpose of the warning. Using isMounted() is a code smell because the only reason you would check is because you think you might be holding a reference after the component has unmounted.

An optimal solution would be to find places where setState() might be called after a component has unmounted, and fix them. Such situations most commonly occur due to callbacks, when a component is waiting for some data and gets unmounted before the data arrives. Ideally, any callbacks should be canceled in componentWillUnmount(), prior to unmounting.

Question: What are the Pointer Events supported in React?

Pointer Events provide a unified way of handling all input events. In the olden days we have a mouse and respective event listeners to handle them but nowadays we have many devices which don't correlate to having a mouse, like phones with touch surface or pens. We need to remember that these events will only work in browsers that support the Pointer Events specification.

The following event types are now available in React DOM:

onPointerDown

onPointerMove

onPointerUp

onPointerCancel

onGotPointerCapture

onLostPointerCaptur

onPointerEnter

onPointerLeave

onPointerOver

onPointerOut

Question: Why should component names start with capital letter?

If you are rendering your component using JSX, the name of that component has to begin with a capital letter otherwise React will throw an error as unrecognized tag. This convention is because only HTML elements and SVG tags can begin with a lowercase letter.

You can define component class which name starts with lowercase letter, but when it's imported it should have capital letter. Here lowercase is fine:

```
class myComponent extends Component {

  render() {   return <div />  }}

export default myComponent
```

While when imported in another file it should start with capital letter:

```
import MyComponent from './MyComponent'
```

Question: Are custom DOM attributes supported in React v16?

Yes. In the past, React used to ignore unknown DOM attributes. If you wrote JSX with an attribute that React doesn't recognize, React would just skip it. For example, this:

```
<div mycustomattribute={'something'} />
```

Would render an empty div to the DOM with React v15:

```
<div />
```

In React v16 any unknown attributes will end up in the DOM:

```
<div mycustomattribute='something' />
```

This is useful for supplying browser-specific non-standard attributes, trying new DOM APIs, and integrating with opinionated third-party libraries.

Question: What is difference between constructor and getInitialState?

You should initialize state in the constructor when using ES6 classes, and getInitialState() method when using React.createClass().

Using ES6 classes:

```
class MyComponent extends React.Component {
  constructor(props) {   super(props)   this.state = { /* initial state */ } }}
```

Using React.createClass():

```
const MyComponent = React.createClass({
  getInitialState() {   return { /* initial state */ } }})
```

Note: React.createClass() is deprecated and removed in React v16. Use plain JavaScript classes instead.

Question: Can you force a component to re-render without calling setState?

By default, when your component's state or props change, your component will re-render. If your render() method depends on some other data, you can tell React that the component needs re-rendering by calling forceUpdate().

```
component.forceUpdate(callback)
```

It is recommended to avoid all uses of forceUpdate() and only read from this.props and this.state in render().

Question: What is the difference between super() and super(props) in React using ES6 classes?

When you want to access this.props in constructor() then you should pass props to super() method.

Using super(props):

```
class MyComponent extends React.Component {
  constructor(props) {   super(props)   console.log(this.props) // { name: 'John', ... } }}
```

Using super():

```
class MyComponent extends React.Component {
  constructor(props) {   super()

    console.log(this.props) // undefined  }}
```

Outside constructor() both will display same value for this.props.

Question: How to loop inside JSX?

You can simply use Array.prototype.map with ES6 arrow function syntax. For example, the items array of objects is mapped into an array of components:

```
<tbody>

  {items.map(item => <SomeComponent key={item.id} name={item.name} />)}

</tbody>
```

You can't iterate using for loop:

```
<tbody>

  for (let i = 0; i < items.length; i++) {

    <SomeComponent key={items[i].id} name={items[i].name} />

  }

</tbody>
```

This is because JSX tags are transpiled into function calls, and you can't use statements inside expressions. This may change thanks to do expressions which are stage 1 proposal.

Question: How do you access props in attribute quotes?

React (or JSX) doesn't support variable interpolation inside an attribute value. The below representation won't work:

```
<img className='image' src='images/{this.props.image}' />
```

But you can put any JS expression inside curly braces as the entire attribute value. So the below expression works:

```
<img className='image' src={'images/' + this.props.image} />
```

Using template strings will also work:

```
<img className='image' src={`images/${this.props.image}`} />
```

Question: What is React proptype array with shape?

If you want to pass an array of objects to a component with a particular shape then use React.PropTypes.shape() as an argument to React.PropTypes.arrayOf().

```
ReactComponent.propTypes = {
```

arrayWithShape: React.PropTypes.arrayOf(React.PropTypes.shape({

  color: React.PropTypes.string.isRequired,

  fontSize: React.PropTypes.number.isRequired

})).isRequired

}

Question: How conditionally apply class attributes?

You shouldn't use curly braces inside quotes because it is going to be evaluated as a string.

<div className="btn-panel {this.props.visible ? 'show' : 'hidden'}">

Instead you need to move curly braces outside (don't forget to include spaces between class names):

<div className={'btn-panel ' + (this.props.visible ? 'show' : 'hidden')}>

Template strings will also work:

<div className={`btn-panel ${this.props.visible ? 'show' : 'hidden'}`}>

Question: What is the difference between React and ReactDOM?

The react package contains React.createElement(), React.Component, React.Children, and other helpers related to elements and component classes. You can think of these as the isomorphic or universal helpers that you need to build components. The react-dom package contains ReactDOM.render(), and in react-dom/server we have server-side rendering support with ReactDOMServer.renderToString() and ReactDOMServer.renderToStaticMarkup().

Question: Why ReactDOM is separated from React?

The React team worked on extracting all DOM-related features into a separate library called ReactDOM. React v0.14 is the first release in which the libraries are split. By looking at some of the packages, react-native, react-art, react-canvas, and react-three, it has become clear that the beauty and essence of React has nothing to do with browsers or the DOM. To build more environments that React can render to, React team planned to split the main React package into two: react and react-dom. This paves the way to writing components that can be shared between the web version of React and React Native.

Question: How to use React label element?

If you try to render a <label> element bound to a text input using the standard for attribute, then it produces HTML missing that attribute and prints a warning to the console.

```jsx
<label for={'user'}>{'User'}</label>
<input type={'text'} id={'user'} />
```

Since for is a reserved keyword in JavaScript, use htmlFor instead.

```jsx
<label htmlFor={'user'}>{'User'}</label>
<input type={'text'} id={'user'} />
```

Question: How to combine multiple inline style objects?

You can use spread operator in regular React:

```jsx
<button style={{...styles.panel.button, ...styles.panel.submitButton}}>{'Submit'}</button>
```

If you're using React Native then you can use the array notation:

```jsx
<button style={[styles.panel.button, styles.panel.submitButton]}>{'Submit'}</button>
```

Question: How to re-render the view when the browser is resized?

You can listen to the resize event in componentDidMount() and then update the dimensions (width and height). You should remove the listener in componentWillUnmount() method.

```jsx
class WindowDimensions extends React.Component {

  componentWillMount() {   this.updateDimensions()  }

  componentDidMount() {   window.addEventListener('resize', this.updateDimensions)  }

  componentWillUnmount() {   window.removeEventListener('resize', this.updateDimensions)  }

  updateDimensions() {   this.setState({width: $(window).width(), height: $(window).height()})  }

  render() {   return <span>{this.state.width} x {this.state.height}</span>  }}
```

Question: What is the difference between setState() and replaceState() methods?

When you use setState() the current and previous states are merged. replaceState() throws out the current state, and replaces it with only what you provide. Usually setState() is used unless you really need to remove all previous keys for some reason. You can also set state to false/null in setState() instead of using replaceState().

Question: How to listen to state changes?

The following lifecycle methods will be called when state changes. You can compare provided state and props values with current state and props to determine if something meaningful changed.

componentWillUpdate(object nextProps, object nextState)

componentDidUpdate(object prevProps, object prevState)

What is the recommended approach of removing an array element in React state?

The better approach is to use Array.prototype.filter() method.

For example, let's create a removeItem() method for updating the state.

removeItem(index) { this.setState({   data: this.state.data.filter((item, i) => i !== index) })}

Question: Is it possible to use React without rendering HTML?

It is possible with latest version (>=16.2). Below are the possible options:

render() { return false}

render() { return null}

render() { return []}

render() { return <React.Fragment></React.Fragment>}

render() { return <></>}

Returning undefined won't work.

Question: How to pretty print JSON with React?

We can use <pre> tag so that the formatting of the JSON.stringify() is retained:

const data = { name: 'John', age: 42 }

class User extends React.Component {

  render() {   return (<pre>   {JSON.stringify(data, null, 2)}   </pre>) }}

React.render(<User />, document.getElementById('container'))

Question: Why you can't update props in React?

The React philosophy is that props should be immutable and top-down. This means that a parent can send any prop values to a child, but the child can't modify received props.

Question: How to focus an input element on page load?

You can do it by creating ref for input element and using it in componentDidMount():

```jsx
class App extends React.Component{
  componentDidMount() {   this.nameInput.focus()  }
  render() {   return (
    <div>    <input      defaultValue={'Won\'t focus'}    />
      <input     ref={(input) => this.nameInput = input}     defaultValue={'Will focus'}     />
    </div>   ) }}

ReactDOM.render(<App />, document.getElementById('app'))
```

Question: What are the possible ways of updating objects in state?

Calling setState() with an object to merge with state:

Using Object.assign() to create a copy of the object:

```jsx
const user = Object.assign({}, this.state.user, { age: 42 })

this.setState({ user })
```

Using spread operator:

```jsx
const user = { ...this.state.user, age: 42 }

this.setState({ user })
```

Calling setState() with a function:

```jsx
this.setState(prevState => ({

  user: {

    ...prevState.user,

    age: 42

  }}))
```

Question: Why function is preferred over object for setState()?

React may batch multiple setState() calls into a single update for performance. Because this.props and this.state may be updated asynchronously, you should not rely on their values for calculating the next state.

This counter example will fail to update as expected:

// Wrong

this.setState({ counter: this.state.counter + this.props.increment, })

The preferred approach is to call setState() with function rather than object. That function will receive the previous state as the first argument, and the props at the time the update is applied as the second argument.

// Correct

this.setState((prevState, props) => ({ counter: prevState.counter + props.increment}))

Question: How can we find the version of React at runtime in the browser?

You can use React.version to get the version.

const REACT_VERSION = React.version

ReactDOM.render(<div>{`React version: ${REACT_VERSION}`}</div>, document.getElementById('app'))

Question: What are the approaches to include polyfills in your create-react-app?

Manual import from core-js:

Create a file called (something like) polyfills.js and import it into root index.js file. Run npm install core-js or yarn add core-js and import your specific required features.

import 'core-js/fn/array/find'

import 'core-js/fn/array/includes'

import 'core-js/fn/number/is-nan'

Using Polyfill service:

Use the polyfill.io CDN to retrieve custom, browser-specific polyfills by adding this line to index.html:

<script src='https://cdn.polyfill.io/v2/polyfill.min.js?features=default,Array.prototype.includes'></script>

In the above script we had to explicitly request the Array.prototype.includes feature as it is not included in the default feature set.

Question: How to use https instead of http in create-react-app?

You just need to use HTTPS=true configuration. You can edit your package.json scripts section:

"scripts": { "start": "set HTTPS=true && react-scripts start"}

or just run set HTTPS=true && npm start

Question: How to avoid using relative path imports in create-react-app?

Create a file called .env in the project root and write the import path:

NODE_PATH=src/app

After that restart the development server. Now you should be able to import anything inside src/app without relative paths.

Question: How to add Google Analytics for React Router?

Add a listener on the history object to record each page view:

history.listen(function (location) {

  window.ga('set', 'page', location.pathname + location.search)

  window.ga('send', 'pageview', location.pathname + location.search)}})

Question: How to update a component every second?

You need to use setInterval() to trigger the change, but you also need to clear the timer when the component unmounts to prevent errors and memory leaks.

componentDidMount() { this.interval = setInterval(() => this.setState({ time: Date.now() }), 1000)}

componentWillUnmount() { clearInterval(this.interval)}

Question: How do you apply vendor prefixes to inline styles in React?

React does not apply vendor prefixes automatically. You need to add vendor prefixes manually.

<div style={{ transform: 'rotate(90deg)', WebkitTransform: 'rotate(90deg)',

// note the capital 'W' here

  msTransform: 'rotate(90deg)' // 'ms' is the only lowercase vendor prefix

}} />

Question: How to import and export components using React and ES6?

You should use default for exporting the components

```jsx
import React from 'react'

import User from 'user'

export default class MyProfile extends React.Component {

  render(){   return (     <User type="customer">

     //...

   </User>   ) }}
```

With the export specifier, the MyProfile is going to be the member and exported to this module and the same can be imported without mentioning the name in other components.

Question: Why React component names must begin with a capital letter?

In JSX, lowercase tag names are considered to be HTML tags. However, capitalized and lowercase tag names with a dot (property accessors) aren't.

<component /> compiles to React.createElement('component') (i.e, HTML tag)

<obj.component /> compiles to React.createElement(obj.component)

<Component /> compiles to React.createElement(Component)

Question: Why is a component constructor called only once?

React's reconciliation algorithm assumes that without any information to the contrary, if a custom component appears in the same place on subsequent renders, it's the same component as before, so reuses the previous instance rather than creating a new one.

Question: How to define constants in React?

You can use ES7 static field to define constant.

```jsx
class MyComponent extends React.Component {  static DEFAULT_PAGINATION = 10}
```

Static fields are part of the Class Fields stage 3 proposal.

Question: How to programmatically trigger click event in React?

You could use the ref prop to acquire a reference to the underlying HTMLInputElement object through a callback, store the reference as a class property, then use that reference to later trigger a click from your event handlers using the HTMLElement.click method. This can be done in two steps:

Create ref in render method:

```
<input ref={input => this.inputElement = input} />
```

Apply click event in your event handler:

```
this.inputElement.click()
```

Question: Is it possible to use async/await in plain React?

If you want to use async/await in React, you will need Babel and transform-async-to-generator plugin. React Native ships with Babel and a set of transforms.

Question: What are the common folder structures for React?

There are two common practices for React project file structure.

Grouping by features or routes:

One common way to structure projects is locate CSS, JS, and tests together, grouped by feature or route.

```
common/
├── Avatar.js
├── Avatar.css
├── APIUtils.js
└── APIUtils.test.js
feed/
├── index.js
├── Feed.js
├── Feed.css
├── FeedStory.js
├── FeedStory.test.js
└── FeedAPI.js
profile/
├── index.js
├── Profile.js
```

├─ ProfileHeader.js

├─ ProfileHeader.css

└─ ProfileAPI.js

Grouping by file type:

Another popular way to structure projects is to group similar files together.

api/

├─ APIUtils.js

├─ APIUtils.test.js

├─ ProfileAPI.js

└─ UserAPI.js

components/

├─ Avatar.js

├─ Avatar.css

├─ Feed.js

├─ Feed.css

├─ FeedStory.js

├─ FeedStory.test.js

├─ Profile.js

├─ ProfileHeader.js

└─ ProfileHeader.css

Question: What are the popular packages for animation?

React Transition Group and React Motion are popular animation packages in React ecosystem.

Question: What is the benefit of styles modules?

It is recommended to avoid hard coding style values in components. Any values that are likely to be used across different UI components should be extracted into their own modules.

For example, these styles could be extracted into a separate component:

export const colors = { white, black, blue}

export const space = [0, 8, 16, 32, 64]

And then imported individually in other components:

import { space, colors } from './styles'

Question: What are the popular React-specific linters?

ESLint is a popular JavaScript linter. There are plugins available that analyse specific code styles. One of the most common for React is an npm package called eslint-plugin-react. By default, it will check a number of best practices, with rules checking things from keys in iterators to a complete set of prop types. Another popular plugin is eslint-plugin-jsx-a11y, which will help fix common issues with accessibility. As JSX offers slightly different syntax to regular HTML, issues with alt text and tabindex, for example, will not be picked up by regular plugins.

Question: How to make AJAX call and in which component lifecycle methods should I make an AJAX call?

You can use AJAX libraries such as Axios, jQuery AJAX, and the browser built-in fetch. You should fetch data in the componentDidMount() lifecycle method. This is so you can use setState() to update your component when the data is retrieved.

For example, the employees list fetched from API and set local state:

```jsx
class MyComponent extends React.Component {

  constructor(props) { super(props)

  this.state = {   employees: [],   error: null  } }

  componentDidMount() {

  fetch('https://api.example.com/items')

    .then(res => res.json())   .then(   (result) => {   this.setState({

      employees: result.employees   })   },   (error) => {   this.setState({ error })   }   ) }

  render() {   const { error, employees } = this.state

  if (error) {   return <div>Error: {error.message}</div>;

  } else {   return (   <ul>   {employees.map(item => (

  <li key={employee.name}>   {employee.name}-{employees.experience}   </li>   ))}
  </ul>   )   } }}
```

Question: What are render props?

Render Props is a simple technique for sharing code between components using a prop whose value is a function. The below component uses render prop which returns a React element.

```
<DataProvider render={data => ( <h1>{`Hello ${data.target}`}</h1>)}/>
```

Libraries such as React Router and DownShift are using this pattern.

React Router

Question: What is React Router?

React Router is a powerful routing library built on top of React that helps you add new screens and flows to your application incredibly quickly, all while keeping the URL in sync with what's being displayed on the page.

Question: How React Router is different from history library?

React Router is a wrapper around the history library which handles interaction with the browser's window.history with its browser and hash histories. It also provides memory history which is useful for environments that don't have global history, such as mobile app development (React Native) and unit testing with Node.

Question: What are the <Router> components of React Router v4?

React Router v4 provides below 3 <Router> components:

```
<BrowserRouter>

<HashRouter>

<MemoryRouter>
```

The above components will create browser, hash, and memory history instances. React Router v4 makes the properties and methods of the history instance associated with your router available through the context in the router object.

Question: What is the purpose of push() and replace() methods of history?

A history instance has two methods for navigation purpose.

```
push()

replace()
```

If you think of the history as an array of visited locations, push() will add a new location to the array and replace() will replace the current location in the array with the new one.

Question: How do you programmatically navigate using React Router v4?

There are three different ways to achieve programmatic routing/navigation within components.

Using the withRouter() higher-order function:

The withRouter() higher-order function will inject the history object as a prop of the component. This object provides push() and replace() methods to avoid the usage of context.

```
import { withRouter } from 'react-router-dom' // this also works with 'react-router-native'

const Button = withRouter(({ history }) => ( <button  type='button'  onClick={() => {
history.push('/new-location') }} >   {'Click Me!'} </button>))
```

Using <Route> component and render props pattern:

The <Route> component passes the same props as withRouter(), so you will be able to access the history methods through the history prop.

```
import { Route } from 'react-router-dom'

const Button = () => ( <Route render={(({ history }) => (   <button     type='button'

   onClick={() => { history.push('/new-location') }}   >    {'Click Me!'}   </button> )} />)
```

Using context:

This option is not recommended and treated as unstable API.

```
const Button = (props, context) => (

  <button   type='button'  onClick={() => { context.history.push('/new-location')   }} >

   {'Click Me!'}  </button> )

Button.contextTypes = {  history: React.PropTypes.shape({  push: React.PropTypes.func.isRequired

 }) }
```

Question: How to get query parameters in React Router v4?

The ability to parse query strings was taken out of React Router v4 because there have been user requests over the years to support different implementation. So the decision has been given to users to choose the implementation they like. The recommended approach is to use query strings library.

const queryString = require('query-string');

const parsed = queryString.parse(props.location.search);

You can also use URLSearchParams if you want something native:

const params = new URLSearchParams(props.location.search)

const foo = params.get('name')

You should use a polyfill for IE11.

Question: Why you get "Router may have only one child element" warning?

You have to wrap your Route's in a <Switch> block because <Switch> is unique in that it renders a route exclusively.

At first you need to add Switch to your imports:

import { Switch, Router, Route } from 'react-router'

Then define the routes within <Switch> block:

<Router>

  <Switch>

    <Route {/* ... */} />

    <Route {/* ... */} />

  </Switch>

</Router>

Question: How to pass params to history.push method in React Router v4?

While navigating you can pass props to the history object:

this.props.history.push({ pathname: '/template', search: '?name=sudheer', state: { detail: response.data } })

The search property is used to pass query params in push() method.

Question: How to implement default or NotFound page?

A <Switch> renders the first child <Route> that matches. A <Route> with no path always matches. So you just need to simply drop path attribute as below

```jsx
<Switch>  <Route exact path="/" component={Home}/>  <Route path="/user" component={User}/>

  <Route component={NotFound} /> </Switch>
```

Question: How to get history on React Router v4?

Create a module that exports a history object and import this module across the project.

For example, create history.js file:

```jsx
import { createBrowserHistory } from 'history'

export default createBrowserHistory({

  /* pass a configuration object here if needed */

})
```

You should use the <Router> component instead of built-in routers. Imported the above history.js inside index.js file:

```jsx
import { Router } from 'react-router-dom'

import history from './history'

import App from './App'

ReactDOM.render(( <Router history={history}>   <App />  </Router> ), holder)
```

You can also use push method of history object similar to built-in history object:

```jsx
// some-other-file.js

import history from './history'

history.push('/go-here')
```

Question: How to perform automatic redirect after login?

The react-router package provides <Redirect> component in React Router. Rendering a <Redirect> will navigate to a new location. Like server-side redirects, the new location will override the current location in the history stack.

```jsx
import React, { Component } from 'react'

import { Redirect } from 'react-router'

export default class LoginComponent extends Component {
```

```
render() {

  if (this.state.isLoggedIn === true) {    return <Redirect to="/your/redirect/page" />   } else {

    return <div>{'Login Please'}</div>    } } }
```

React Internationalization

Question: What is React Intl?

The React Intl library makes internalization in React straightforward, with off-the-shelf components and an API that can handle everything from formatting strings, dates, and numbers, to pluralization. React Intl is part of FormatJS which provides bindings to React via its components and API.

Question: What are the main features of React Intl?

Display numbers with separators.

Display dates and times correctly.

Display dates relative to "now".

Pluralize labels in strings.

Support for 150+ languages.

Runs in the browser and Node.

Built on standards.

Question: What are the two ways of formatting in React Intl?

The library provides two ways to format strings, numbers, and dates: react components or an API.

```
<FormattedMessage id={'account'} defaultMessage={'The amount is less than minimum balance.'}/>

const messages = defineMessages({ accountMessage: { id: 'account', defaultMessage: 'The amount is less than minimum balance.', } })

formatMessage(messages.accountMessage)
```

Question: How to use <FormattedMessage> as placeholder using React Intl?

The <Formatted... /> components from react-intl return elements, not plain text, so they can't be used for placeholders, alt text, etc. In that case, you should use lower level API formatMessage(). You can inject the intl object into your component using injectIntl() higher-order component and then format the message using formatMessage() available on that object.

```
import React from 'react'

import { injectIntl, intlShape } from 'react-intl'

const MyComponent = ({ intl }) => {  const placeholder = intl.formatMessage({id: 'messageId'})

  return <input placeholder={placeholder} />  }

MyComponent.propTypes = {  intl: intlShape.isRequired }

export default injectIntl(MyComponent)
```

Question: How to access current locale with React Intl?

You can get the current locale in any component of your application using injectIntl():

```
import { injectIntl, intlShape } from 'react-intl'

const MyComponent = ({ intl }) => (

  <div>{`The current locale is ${intl.locale}`}</div>  )

MyComponent.propTypes = {  intl: intlShape.isRequired  }

export default injectIntl(MyComponent)
```

Question: How to format date using React Intl?

The injectIntl() higher-order component will give you access to the formatDate() method via the props in your component. The method is used internally by instances of FormattedDate and it returns the string representation of the formatted date.

```
import { injectIntl, intlShape } from 'react-intl'

const stringDate = this.props.intl.formatDate(date, {  year: 'numeric',  month: 'numeric', day: 'numeric' })

const MyComponent = ({intl}) => (  <div>{`The formatted date is ${stringDate}`}</div> )

MyComponent.propTypes = {  intl: intlShape.isRequired  }

export default injectIntl(MyComponent)
```

React Testing

Question: What is Shallow Renderer in React testing?

Shallow rendering is useful for writing unit test cases in React. It lets you render a component one level deep and assert facts about what its render method returns, without worrying about the behavior of child components, which are not instantiated or rendered.

For example, if you have the following component:

```
function MyComponent() {

  return (    <div> <span className={'heading'}>{'Title'}</span>

<span className={'description'}>{'Description'}</span>   </div> ) }
```

Then you can assert as follows:

```
import ShallowRenderer from 'react-test-renderer/shallow'

// in your test

const renderer = new ShallowRenderer()

renderer.render(<MyComponent />)

const result = renderer.getRenderOutput()

expect(result.type).toBe('div')

expect(result.props.children).toEqual([

  <span className={'heading'}>{'Title'}</span>,

<span className={'description'}>{'Description'}</span>   ])
```

Question: What is TestRenderer package in React?

This package provides a renderer that can be used to render components to pure JavaScript objects, without depending on the DOM or a native mobile environment. This package makes it easy to grab a snapshot of the platform view hierarchy (similar to a DOM tree) rendered by a ReactDOM or React Native without using a browser or jsdom.

```
import TestRenderer from 'react-test-renderer'

const Link = ({page, children}) => <a href={page}>{children}</a>

const testRenderer = TestRenderer.create(

  <Link page={'https://www.facebook.com/'}>{'Facebook'}</Link> )

console.log(testRenderer.toJSON())

// {
```

```
//   type: 'a',

//   props: { href: 'https://www.facebook.com/' },

//   children: [ 'Facebook' ]

// }
```

Question: What is the purpose of ReactTestUtils package?

ReactTestUtils are provided in the with-addons package and allow you to perform actions against a simulated DOM for the purpose of unit testing.

Question: What is Jest?

Jest is a JavaScript unit testing framework created by Facebook based on Jasmine and provides automated mock creation and a jsdom environment. It's often used for testing components.

Question: What are the advantages of Jest over Jasmine?

There are couple of advantages compared to Jasmine:

Automatically finds tests to execute in your source code.

Automatically mocks dependencies when running your tests.

Allows you to test asynchronous code synchronously.

Runs your tests with a fake DOM implementation (via jsdom) so that your tests can be run on the command line.

Runs tests in parallel processes so that they finish sooner.

Give a simple example of Jest test case

Let's write a test for a function that adds two numbers in sum.js file:

```
const sum = (a, b) => a + b

export default sum
```

Create a file named sum.test.js which contains actual test:

```
import sum from './sum'

test('adds 1 + 2 to equal 3', () => { expect(sum(1, 2)).toBe(3) })
```

And then add the following section to your package.json:

```
{ "scripts": { "test": "jest" } }
```

Finally, run yarn test or npm test and Jest will print a result:

```
$ yarn test

PASS ./sum.test.js

✓ adds 1 + 2 to equal 3 (2ms)
```

React Redux

Question: What is flux?

Flux is an application design paradigm used as a replacement for the more traditional MVC pattern. It is not a framework or a library but a new kind of architecture that complements React and the concept of Unidirectional Data Flow. Facebook uses this pattern internally when working with React.

The workflow between dispatcher, stores and views components with distinct inputs and outputs as follows: flux

Question: What is Redux?

Redux is a predictable state container for JavaScript apps based on the Flux design pattern. Redux can be used together with React, or with any other view library. It is tiny (about 2kB) and has no dependencies.

Question: What are the core principles of Redux?

Redux follows three fundamental principles:

Single source of truth: The state of your whole application is stored in an object tree within a single store. The single state tree makes it easier to keep track of changes over time and debug or inspect the application.

State is read-only: The only way to change the state is to emit an action, an object describing what happened. This ensures that neither the views nor the network callbacks will ever write directly to the state.

Changes are made with pure functions: To specify how the state tree is transformed by actions, you write reducers. Reducers are just pure functions that take the previous state and an action as parameters, and return the next state.

Question: What are the downsides of Redux compared to Flux?

Instead of saying downsides we can say that there are few compromises of using Redux over Flux.

Those are as follows:

You will need to learn to avoid mutations: Flux is un-opinionated about mutating data, but Redux doesn't like mutations and many packages complementary to Redux assume you never mutate the state. You can enforce this with dev-only packages like redux-immutable-state-invariant, Immutable.js, or instructing your team to write non-mutating code.

You're going to have to carefully pick your packages: While Flux explicitly doesn't try to solve problems such as undo/redo, persistence, or forms, Redux has extension points such as middleware and store enhancers, and it has spawned a rich ecosystem.

There is no nice Flow integration yet: Flux currently lets you do very impressive static type checks which Redux doesn't support yet.

Question: What is the difference between mapStateToProps() and mapDispatchToProps()?

mapStateToProps() is a utility which helps your component get updated state (which is updated by some other components):

const mapStateToProps = (state) => { return {   todos: getVisibleTodos(state.todos, state.visibilityFilter) } }

mapDispatchToProps() is a utility which will help your component to fire an action event (dispatching action which may cause change of application state):

const mapDispatchToProps = (dispatch) => { return {   onTodoClick: (id) => { dispatch(toggleTodo(id)) } } }

Question: Can I dispatch an action in reducer?

Dispatching an action within a reducer is an anti-pattern. Your reducer should be without side effects, simply digesting the action payload and returning a new state object. Adding listeners and dispatching actions within the reducer can lead to chained actions and other side effects.

Question: How to access Redux store outside a component?

Yes. You just need to export the store from the module where it created with createStore(). Also, it shouldn't pollute the global window object.

store = createStore(myReducer)

export default store

Question: What are the drawbacks of MVW pattern?

The DOM manipulation is very expensive which causes applications behaves slowly and inefficient.

Due to circular dependencies, a complicated model was created around models and views.

Lot of data changes happens for collaborative applications(like Google Docs).

No way to do undo (travel back in time) easily without adding so much extra code.

Question: Are there any similarities between Redux and RxJS?

These libraries are very different for very different purposes, but there are some vague similarities.

Redux is a tool for managing state throughout the application. It is usually used as an architecture for UIs. Think of it as an alternative to (half of) Angular. RxJS is a reactive programming library. It is usually used as a tool to accomplish asynchronous tasks in JavaScript. Think of it as an alternative to Promises. Redux uses the Reactive paradigm because the Store is reactive. The Store observes actions from a distance, and changes itself. RxJS also uses the Reactive paradigm, but instead of being an architecture, it gives you basic building blocks, Observables, to accomplish this pattern.

Question: How to dispatch an action on load?

You can dispatch an action in componentDidMount() method and in render() method you can verify the data.

```
class App extends Component {

  componentDidMount() {   this.props.fetchData()}

  render() {   return this.props.isLoaded  ? <div>{'Loaded'}</div> : <div>{'Not Loaded'}</div> } }

const mapStateToProps = (state) => ({ isLoaded: state.isLoaded })

const mapDispatchToProps = { fetchData }

export default connect(mapStateToProps, mapDispatchToProps)(App)
```

Question: How to use connect() from React Redux?

You need to follow two steps to use your store in your container:

Use mapStateToProps(): It maps the state variables from your store to the props that you specify.

Connect the above props to your container: The object returned by the mapStateToProps function is connected to the container. You can import connect() from react-redux.

```
import React from 'react'

import { connect } from 'react-redux'

class App extends React.Component {
```

```
render() {   return <div>{this.props.containerData}</div> } }
```

```
function mapStateToProps(state) {  return { containerData: state.data } }
```

```
export default connect(mapStateToProps)(App)
```

Question: How to reset state in Redux?

You need to write a root reducer in your application which delegate handling the action to the reducer generated by combineReducers().

For example, let us take rootReducer() to return the initial state after USER_LOGOUT action. As we know, reducers are supposed to return the initial state when they are called with undefined as the first argument, no matter the action.

```
const appReducer = combineReducers({

  /* your app's top-level reducers */

})
```

```
const rootReducer = (state, action) => {  if (action.type === 'USER_LOGOUT') { state = undefined  }

  return appReducer(state, action) }
```

In case of using redux-persist, you may also need to clean your storage. redux-persist keeps a copy of your state in a storage engine. First, you need to import the appropriate storage engine and then, to parse the state before setting it to undefined and clean each storage state key.

```
const appReducer = combineReducers({

  /* your app's top-level reducers */

})
```

```
const rootReducer = (state, action) => {  if (action.type === 'USER_LOGOUT') {

    Object.keys(state).forEach(key => {    storage.removeItem(`persist:${key}`)   })

    state = undefined  } return appReducer(state, action) }
```

Question: Whats the purpose of at symbol in the Redux connect decorator?

The @ symbol is in fact a JavaScript expression used to signify decorators. Decorators make it possible to annotate and modify classes and properties at design time.

Let's take an example setting up Redux without and with a decorator.

Without decorator:

```
import React from 'react'

import * as actionCreators from './actionCreators'

import { bindActionCreators } from 'redux'

import { connect } from 'react-redux'

function mapStateToProps(state) {  return { todos: state.todos } }

function mapDispatchToProps(dispatch) {   return { actions: bindActionCreators(actionCreators, dispatch) }}

class MyApp extends React.Component {

  // ...define your main app here

}

export default connect(mapStateToProps, mapDispatchToProps)(MyApp)
```

With decorator:

```
import React from 'react'

import * as actionCreators from './actionCreators'

import { bindActionCreators } from 'redux'

import { connect } from 'react-redux'

function mapStateToProps(state) {  return { todos: state.todos } }

function mapDispatchToProps(dispatch) {  return { actions: bindActionCreators(actionCreators, dispatch) } }

@connect(mapStateToProps, mapDispatchToProps)

export default class MyApp extends React.Component {

  // ...define your main app here

}
```

The above examples are almost similar except the usage of decorator. The decorator syntax isn't built into any JavaScript runtimes yet, and is still experimental and subject to change. You can use babel for the decorators support.

Question: What is the difference between React context and React Redux?

You can use Context in your application directly and is going to be great for passing down data to deeply nested components which what it was designed for. Whereas Redux is much more powerful and provides a large number of features that the Context API doesn't provide. Also, React Redux uses context internally but it doesn't expose this fact in the public API.

Question: Why are Redux state functions called reducers?

Reducers always return the accumulation of the state (based on all previous and current actions). Therefore, they act as a reducer of state. Each time a Redux reducer is called, the state and action are passed as parameters. This state is then reduced (or accumulated) based on the action, and then the next state is returned. You could reduce a collection of actions and an initial state (of the store) on which to perform these actions to get the resulting final state.

Question: How to make AJAX request in Redux?

You can use redux-thunk middleware which allows you to define async actions.

Let's take an example of fetching specific account as an AJAX call using fetch API:

export function fetchAccount(id) { return dispatch => {

   dispatch(setLoadingAccountState()) // Show a loading spinner

   fetch(`/account/${id}`, (response) => {   dispatch(doneFetchingAccount()) // Hide loading spinner

      if (response.status === 200) {   dispatch(setAccount(response.json)) // Use a normal function to set the received state

   } else {   dispatch(someError)   }   })   }}

function setAccount(data) { return { type: 'SET_Account', data: data } }

Question: Should I keep all component's state in Redux store?

Keep your data in the Redux store, and the UI related state internally in the component.

Question: What is the proper way to access Redux store?

The best way to access your store in a component is to use the connect() function, that creates a new component that wraps around your existing one. This pattern is called Higher-Order Components, and is generally the preferred way of extending a component's functionality in React. This allows you to map state and action creators to your component, and have them passed in automatically as your store updates.

Let's take an example of <FilterLink> component using connect:

```
import { connect } from 'react-redux'

import { setVisibilityFilter } from '../actions'

import Link from '../components/Link'

const mapStateToProps = (state, ownProps) => ({active: ownProps.filter === state.visibilityFilter})

const mapDispatchToProps = (dispatch, ownProps) => ({ onClick: () =>
dispatch(setVisibilityFilter(ownProps.filter)) })

const FilterLink = connect( mapStateToProps,  mapDispatchToProps )(Link)

export default FilterLink
```

Due to it having quite a few performance optimizations and generally being less likely to cause bugs, the Redux developers almost always recommend using connect() over accessing the store directly (using context API).

```
class MyComponent {  someMethod() {  doSomethingWith(this.context.store)  } }
```

Question: What is the difference between component and container in React Redux?

Component is a class or function component that describes the presentational part of your application.

Container is an informal term for a component that is connected to a Redux store. Containers subscribe to Redux state updates and dispatch actions, and they usually don't render DOM elements; they delegate rendering to presentational child components.

Question: What is the purpose of the constants in Redux?

Constants allows you to easily find all usages of that specific functionality across the project when you use an IDE. It also prevents you from introducing silly bugs caused by typos – in which case, you will get a ReferenceError immediately.

Normally we will save them in a single file (constants.js or actionTypes.js).

```
export const ADD_TODO = 'ADD_TODO'

export const DELETE_TODO = 'DELETE_TODO'

export const EDIT_TODO = 'EDIT_TODO'

export const COMPLETE_TODO = 'COMPLETE_TODO'
```

export const COMPLETE_ALL = 'COMPLETE_ALL'

export const CLEAR_COMPLETED = 'CLEAR_COMPLETED'

In Redux you use them in two places:

During action creation:

Let's take actions.js:

```
import { ADD_TODO } from './actionTypes';

export function addTodo(text) { return { type: ADD_TODO, text } }
```

In reducers:

Let's create reducer.js:

```
import { ADD_TODO } from './actionTypes'

export default (state = [], action) => { switch (action.type) {

  case ADD_TODO:

    return [    ...state,    {    text: action.text,    completed: false    }   ];

  default:    return state  }}
```

Question: What are the different ways to write mapDispatchToProps()?

There are a few ways of binding action creators to dispatch() in mapDispatchToProps(). Below are the possible options:

```
const mapDispatchToProps = (dispatch) => ({  action: () => dispatch(action()) })

const mapDispatchToProps = (dispatch) => ({  action: bindActionCreators(action, dispatch) })

const mapDispatchToProps = { action }
```

The third option is just a shorthand for the first one.

Question: What is the use of the ownProps parameter in mapStateToProps() and mapDispatchToProps()?

If the ownProps parameter is specified, React Redux will pass the props that were passed to the component into your connect functions. So, if you use a connected component:

```
import ConnectedComponent from './containers/ConnectedComponent';
```

```
<ConnectedComponent user={'john'} />
```

The ownProps inside your mapStateToProps() and mapDispatchToProps() functions will be an object:

```
{ user: 'john' }
```

You can use this object to decide what to return from those functions.

Question: How to structure Redux top level directories?

Most of the applications has several top-level directories as below:

Components: Used for dumb components unaware of Redux.

Containers: Used for smart components connected to Redux.

Actions: Used for all action creators, where file names correspond to part of the app.

Reducers: Used for all reducers, where files name correspond to state key.

Store: Used for store initialization.

This structure works well for small and medium size apps.

Question: What is redux-saga?

redux-saga is a library that aims to make side effects (asynchronous things like data fetching and impure things like accessing the browser cache) in React/Redux applications easier and better.

It is available in NPM:

```
$ npm install --save redux-saga
```

Question: What is the mental model of redux-saga?

Saga is like a separate thread in your application, that's solely responsible for side effects. redux-saga is a redux middleware, which means this thread can be started, paused and cancelled from the main application with normal Redux actions, it has access to the full Redux application state and it can dispatch Redux actions as well.

Question: What are the differences between call() and put() in redux-saga?

Both call() and put() are effect creator functions. call() function is used to create effect description, which instructs middleware to call the promise. put() function creates an effect, which instructs middleware to dispatch an action to the store.

Let's take example of how these effects work for fetching particular user data.

```
function* fetchUserSaga(action) {

  // `call` function accepts rest arguments, which will be passed to `api.fetchUser` function.

  // Instructing middleware to call promise, it resolved value will be assigned to `userData` variable

  const userData = yield call(api.fetchUser, action.userId)

  // Instructing middleware to dispatch corresponding action.

  yield put({   type: 'FETCH_USER_SUCCESS',   userData  })}
```

Question: What is Redux Thunk?

Redux Thunk middleware allows you to write action creators that return a function instead of an action. The thunk can be used to delay the dispatch of an action, or to dispatch only if a certain condition is met. The inner function receives the store methods dispatch() and getState() as parameters.

Question: What are the differences between redux-saga and redux-thunk?

Both Redux Thunk and Redux Saga take care of dealing with side effects. In most of the scenarios, Thunk uses Promises to deal with them, whereas Saga uses Generators. Thunk is simple to use and Promises are familiar to many developers, Sagas/Generators are more powerful but you will need to learn them. But both middleware can coexist, so you can start with Thunks and introduce Sagas when/if you need them.

Question: What is Redux DevTools?

Redux DevTools is a live-editing time travel environment for Redux with hot reloading, action replay, and customizable UI. If you don't want to bother with installing Redux DevTools and integrating it into your project, consider using Redux DevTools Extension for Chrome and Firefox.

Question: What are the features of Redux DevTools?

Lets you inspect every state and action payload.

Lets you go back in time by cancelling actions.

If you change the reducer code, each staged action will be re-evaluated.

If the reducers throw, you will see during which action this happened, and what the error was.

With persistState() store enhancer, you can persist debug sessions across page reloads.

Question: What are Redux selectors and why to use them?

Selectors are functions that take Redux state as an argument and return some data to pass to the component.

For example, to get user details from the state:

const getUserData = state => state.user.data

Question: What is Redux Form?

Redux Form works with React and Redux to enable a form in React to use Redux to store all of its state. Redux Form can be used with raw HTML5 inputs, but it also works very well with common UI frameworks like Material UI, React Widgets and React Bootstrap.

Question: What are the main features of Redux Form?

Field values persistence via Redux store.

Validation (sync/async) and submission.

Formatting, parsing and normalization of field values.

Question: How to add multiple middlewares to Redux?

You can use applyMiddleware().

For example, you can add redux-thunk and logger passing them as arguments to applyMiddleware():

import { createStore, applyMiddleware } from 'redux'

const createStoreWithMiddleware = applyMiddleware(ReduxThunk, logger)(createStore)

Question: How to set initial state in Redux?

You need to pass initial state as second argument to createStore:

const rootReducer = combineReducers({ todos: todos, visibilityFilter: visibilityFilter})

const initialState = { todos: [{ id: 123, name: 'example', completed: false }]}

const store = createStore(rootReducer, initialState)

Question: How Relay is different from Redux?

Relay is similar to Redux in that they both use a single store. The main difference is that relay only manages state originated from the server, and all access to the state is used via GraphQL queries (for reading data) and mutations (for changing data). Relay caches the data for you and optimizes data fetching for you, by fetching only changed data and nothing more.

React Native

Question: What is the difference between React Native and React?

React is a JavaScript library, supporting both front end web and being run on the server, for building user interfaces and web applications.

React Native is a mobile framework that compiles to native app components, allowing you to build native mobile applications (iOS, Android, and Windows) in JavaScript that allows you to use React to build your components, and implements React under the hood.

Question: How to test React Native apps?

React Native can be tested only in mobile simulators like iOS and Android. You can run the app in your mobile using expo app (https://expo.io) Where it syncs using QR code, your mobile and computer should be in same wireless network.

Question: How to do logging in React Native?

You can use console.log, console.warn, etc. As of React Native v0.29 you can simply run the following to see logs in the console:

$ react-native log-ios

$ react-native log-android

Question: How to debug your React Native?

Follow the below steps to debug React Native app:

Run your application in the iOS simulator.

Press Command + D and a webpage should open up at http://localhost:8081/debugger-ui.

Enable Pause On Caught Exceptions for a better debugging experience.

Press Command + Option + I to open the Chrome Developer tools, or open it via View -> Developer -> Developer Tools.

You should now be able to debug as you normally would.

React supported libraries & Integration

Question: What is reselect and how it works?

Reselect is a selector library (for Redux) which uses memoization concept. It was originally written to compute derived data from Redux-like applications state, but it can't be tied to any architecture or library.

Reselect keeps a copy of the last inputs/outputs of the last call, and recomputes the result only if one of the inputs changes. If the same inputs are provided twice in a row, Reselect returns the cached output. It's memoization and cache are fully customizable.

Question: What is Flow?

Flow is a static type checker designed to find type errors in JavaScript. Flow types can express much more fine-grained distinctions than traditional type systems. For example, Flow helps you catch errors involving null, unlike most type systems.

Question: What is the difference between Flow and PropTypes?

Flow is a static analysis tool (static checker) which uses a superset of the language, allowing you to add type annotations to all of your code and catch an entire class of bugs at compile time. PropTypes is a basic type checker (runtime checker) which has been patched onto React. It can't check anything other than the types of the props being passed to a given component. If you want more flexible typechecking for your entire project Flow/TypeScript are appropriate choices.

Question: How to use Font Awesome icons in React?

The below steps followed to include Font Awesome in React:

Install font-awesome:

$ npm install --save font-awesome

Import font-awesome in your index.js file:

import 'font-awesome/css/font-awesome.min.css'

Add Font Awesome classes in className:

render() { return <div><i className={'fa fa-spinner'} /></div>}

Question: What is React Dev Tools?

React Developer Tools let you inspect the component hierarchy, including component props and state. It exists both as a browser extension (for Chrome and Firefox), and as a standalone app (works with other environments including Safari, IE, and React Native).

The official extensions available for different browsers or environments.

Chrome extension

Firefox extension

Standalone app (Safari, React Native, etc)

Why is DevTools not loading in Chrome for local files?

If you opened a local HTML file in your browser (file://...) then you must first open Chrome Extensions and check Allow access to file URLs.

Question: How to use Polymer in React?

Create a Polymer element:

```
<link rel='import' href='../../bower_components/polymer/polymer.html' />

Polymer({ is: 'calender-element',

  ready: function() {   this.textContent = 'I am a calender'  }})
```

Create the Polymer component HTML tag by importing it in a HTML document, e.g. import it in the index.html of your React application:

```
<link rel='import' href='./src/polymer-components/calender-element.html'>
```

Use that element in the JSX file:

```
import React from 'react'

class MyComponent extends React.Component {

  render() {   return (    <calender-element />   ) }}

export default MyComponent
```

Question: What are the advantages of React over Vue.js?

React has the following advantages over Vue.js:

Gives more flexibility in large apps developing.

Easier to test.

Suitable for mobile apps creating.

More information and solutions available.

Question: What is the difference between React and Angular?

React   Angular

React is a library and has only the View layer   Angular is a framework and has complete MVC functionality

React handles rendering on the server side   AngularJS renders only on the client side but Angular 2 and above renders on the server side

React uses JSX that looks like HTML in JS which can be confusing   Angular follows the template approach for HTML, which makes code shorter and easy to understand

React Native, which is a React type to build mobile applications are faster and more stable   Ionic, Angular's mobile native app is relatively less stable and slower

In React, data flows only in one way and hence debugging is easy   In Angular, data flows both way i.e it has two-way data binding between children and parent and hence debugging is often difficult

Question: Why React tab is not showing up in DevTools?

When the page loads, React DevTools sets a global named __REACT_DEVTOOLS_GLOBAL_HOOK__, then React communicates with that hook during initialization. If the website is not using React or if React fails to communicate with DevTools then it won't show up the tab.

Question: What are Styled Components?

styled-components is a JavaScript library for styling React applications. It removes the mapping between styles and components, and lets you write actual CSS augmented with JavaScript.

Question: Give an example of Styled Components?

Lets create <Title> and <Wrapper> components with specific styles for each.

import React from 'react'

import styled from 'styled-components'

// Create a <Title> component that renders an <h1> which is centered, red and sized at 1.5em

const Title = styled.h1`

  font-size: 1.5em;

  text-align: center;

  color: palevioletred;

`

```
// Create a <Wrapper> component that renders a <section> with some padding and a papayawhip
background

const Wrapper = styled.section`

 padding: 4em;

 background: papayawhip;

`
```

These two variables, Title and Wrapper, are now components that you can render just like any other react component.

```
<Wrapper>  <Title>{'Lets start first styled component!'}</Title></Wrapper>
```

Question: What is Relay?

Relay is a JavaScript framework for providing a data layer and client-server communication to web applications using the React view layer.

Question: How to use TypeScript in create-react-app application?

When you create a new project supply --scripts-version option as react-scripts-ts. react-scripts-ts is a set of adjustments to take the standard create-react-app project pipeline and bring TypeScript into the mix.

Now the project layout should look like the following:

```
my-app/
├── .gitignore
├── images.d.ts
├── node_modules/
├── public/
├── src/
│   └── ...
├── package.json
├── tsconfig.json
```

├─ tsconfig.prod.json

├─ tsconfig.test.json

└─ tslint.json

Miscellaneous

Question: What are the main features of Reselect library?

Selectors can compute derived data, allowing Redux to store the minimal possible state.

Selectors are efficient. A selector is not recomputed unless one of its arguments changes.

Selectors are composable. They can be used as input to other selectors.

Question: Give an example of Reselect usage?

Let's take calculations and different amounts of a shipment order with the simplified usage of Reselect:

```
import { createSelector } from 'reselect'

const shopItemsSelector = state => state.shop.items

const taxPercentSelector = state => state.shop.taxPercent

const subtotalSelector = createSelector( shopItemsSelector,  items => items.reduce((acc, item) => acc + item.value, 0) )

const taxSelector = createSelector( subtotalSelector,  taxPercentSelector,  (subtotal, taxPercent) => subtotal * (taxPercent / 100) )

export const totalSelector = createSelector( subtotalSelector,  taxSelector,  (subtotal, tax) => ({ total: subtotal + tax }) )

let exampleState = { shop: {   taxPercent: 8,    items: [     { name: 'apple', value: 1.20 },

   { name: 'orange', value: 0.95 },    ]  }}

console.log(subtotalSelector(exampleState)) // 2.15

console.log(taxSelector(exampleState))    // 0.172

console.log(totalSelector(exampleState))   // { total: 2.322 }
```

Question: What is an action in Redux?

Actions are plain JavaScript objects or payloads of information that send data from your application to your store. They are the only source of information for the store. Actions must have a type property that indicates the type of action being performed.

For example an example action which represents adding a new todo item:

```
{ type: ADD_TODO,

  text: 'Add todo item'}
```

Question: Does the statics object work with ES6 classes in React?

No, statics only works with React.createClass():

```
someComponent= React.createClass({

  statics: {   someMethod: function() {

    // ..

  } } })
```

But you can write statics inside ES6+ classes like this:

```
class Component extends React.Component {

  static propTypes = {

    // ...

  }

  static someMethod() {

    // ...

  } }
```

Question: Can Redux only be used with React?

Redux can be used as a data store for any UI layer. The most common usage is with React and React Native, but there are bindings available for Angular, Angular 2, Vue, Mithril, and more. Redux simply provides a subscription mechanism which can be used by any other code.

Question: Do you need to have a particular build tool to use Redux?

Redux is originally written in ES6 and transpiled for production into ES5 with Webpack and Babel. You should be able to use it regardless of your JavaScript build process. Redux also offers a UMD build that can be used directly without any build process at all.

Question: How Redux Form initialValues get updated from state?

You need to add enableReinitialize : true setting.

const InitializeFromStateForm = reduxForm({ form: 'initializeFromState', enableReinitialize : true })(UserEdit)

If your initialValues prop gets updated, your form will update too.

Question: How React PropTypes allow different types for one prop?

You can use oneOfType() method of PropTypes.

For example, the height property can be defined with either string or number type as below:

Component.PropTypes = { size: PropTypes.oneOfType([PropTypes.string, PropTypes.number]) }

Question: Can I import an SVG file as react component?

You can import SVG directly as component instead of loading it as a file. This feature is available with react-scripts@2.0.0 and higher.

import { ReactComponent as Logo } from './logo.svg'

const App = () => (<div>   {/* Logo is an actual react component */}   <Logo /> </div>)

Note: Don't forget about the curly braces in the import.

Question: Why are inline ref callbacks or functions not recommended?

If the ref callback is defined as an inline function, it will get called twice during updates, first with null and then again with the DOM element. This is because a new instance of the function is created with each render, so React needs to clear the old ref and set up the new one.

class UserForm extends Component {

  handleSubmit = () => {   console.log("Input Value is: ", this.input.value) }

  render () {   return (<form onSubmit={this.handleSubmit}>

    <input   type='text' ref={(input) => this.input = input} /> // Access DOM input in handle submit

    <button type='submit'>Submit</button> </form>) } }

But our expectation is for the ref callback to get called once, when the component mounts. One quick fix is to use the ES7 class property syntax to define the function

```
class UserForm extends Component {  handleSubmit = () => {  console.log("Input Value is: ",
this.input.value) }

setSearchInput = (input) => {   this.input = input  }

render () {  return (<form onSubmit={this.handleSubmit}>

    <input      type='text'  ref={this.setSearchInput} /> // Access DOM input in handle submit

    <button type='submit'>Submit</button> </form> ) } }
```

Question: What is render hijacking in react?

The concept of render hijacking is the ability to control what a component will output from another
component. It actually means that you decorate your component by wrapping it into a Higher-Order
component. By wrapping you can inject additional props or make other changes, which can cause
changing logic of rendering. It does not actually enables hijacking, but by using HOC you make your
component behave in different way.

Question: What are HOC factory implementations?

There are two main ways of implementing HOCs in React. 1. Props Proxy (PP) and 2. Inheritance
Inversion (II). They follow different approaches for manipulating the WrappedComponent. Props
Proxy

In this approach, the render method of the HOC returns a React Element of the type of the
WrappedComponent. We also pass through the props that the HOC receives, hence the name Props
Proxy.

```
function ppHOC(WrappedComponent) {

 return class PP extends React.Component {

  render() {    return <WrappedComponent {...this.props}/> } } }
```

Inheritance Inversion In this approach, the returned HOC class (Enhancer) extends the
WrappedComponent. It is called Inheritance Inversion because instead of the WrappedComponent
extending some Enhancer class, it is passively extended by the Enhancer. In this way the relationship
between them seems inverse.

```
function iiHOC(WrappedComponent) { return class Enhancer extends WrappedComponent {

  render() {    return super.render() } } }
```

Question: How to pass numbers to React component?

You should be passing the numbers via curly braces({}) where as strings inn quotes

    React.render(<User age={30} department={"IT"} />, document.getElementById('container'));

Question: Do I need to keep all my state into Redux? Should I ever use react internal state?

It is up to developer decision. i.e, It is developer job to determine what kinds of state make up your application, and where each piece of state should liveSome users prefer to keep every single piece of data in Redux, to maintain a fully serializable and controlled version of their application at all times. Others prefer to keep non-critical or UI state, such as "is this dropdown currently open", inside a component's internal state.

Below are the thumb rules to determine what kind of data should be put into Redux

Question: Do other parts of the application care about this data?

Question: Do you need to be able to create further derived data based on this original data?

Question: Is the same data being used to drive multiple components?

Question: Is there value to you in being able to restore this state to a given point in time (ie, time travel debugging)?

Question: Do you want to cache the data (ie, use what's in state if it's already there instead of re-requesting it)?

Question: What is the purpose of registerServiceWorker in React?

React creates a service worker for you without any configuration by default. The service worker is a web API that helps you cache your assets and other files so that when the user is offline or on slow network, he/she can still see results on the screen, as such, it helps you build a better user experience, that's what you should know about service worker's for now. It's all about adding offline capabilities to your site.

    import React from 'react';

    import ReactDOM from 'react-dom';

    import App from './App';

    import registerServiceWorker from './registerServiceWorker';

    ReactDOM.render(<App />, document.getElementById('root'));

    registerServiceWorker();

Question: What is React memo funtion?

Class components can be restricted from rendering when their input props are the same using PureComponent or shouldComponentUpdate. Now you can do the same with function components by wrapping them in React.memo.

const MyComponent = React.memo(function MyComponent(props) {

 /* only rerenders if props change */

});

Question: What is React lazy function?

The React.lazy function lets you render an dynamic import as a regular component. It will automatically load the bundle containing the OtherComponent when the component gets rendered. This must return a Promise which resolves to a module with a default export containing a React component.

const OtherComponent = React.lazy(() => import('./OtherComponent'));

function MyComponent() { return (

  <div>   <OtherComponent /> </div>); }

Note: React.lazy and Suspense is not yet available for server-side rendering. If you want to do code-splitting in a server rendered app, we still recommend React Loadable.

Question: How to prevent unnecessary updates using setState?

You can compare current value of the state with an existing state value and decide whether to rerender the page or not. If the values are same then you need to return null to stop rerendering otherwise return the latest state value. For example, the user profile information is conditionally rendered as follows,

getUserProfile = user => { const latestAddress = user.address;

  this.setState(state => {   if (state.address === latestAddress) {

    return null;   } else {   return { title: latestAddress };   } }); };

Question: How do you render Array, Strings and Numbers in React 16 Version?

Arrays: Unlike older releases, you don't need to make sure render method return a single element in React16. You are able to return multiple sibling elements without a wrapping element by returning an array. For example, let us take the below list of developers,

```jsx
const ReactJSDevs = () => {

  return [   <li key="1">John</li>, <li key="2">Jackie</li>, <li key="3">Jordan</li> ];}
```

You can also merge this array of items in another array component

```jsx
const JSDevs = () => {

  return (   <ul> <li>Brad</li>   <li>Brodge</li> <ReactJSDevs/> <li>Brandon</li> </ul> ); }
```

Strings and Numbers: You can also return string and number type from the render method

```jsx
render() { return 'Welcome to ReactJS questions'; }
```

```jsx
// Number

render() { return 2018; }
```

Question: How to use class field declarations syntax in React classes?

React Class Components can be made much more concise using the class field declarations. You can initialize local state without using the constructor and declare class methods by using arrow functions without the extra need to bind them. Let's take a counter example to demonstrate class field declarations for state without using constructor and methods without binding,

```jsx
class Counter extends Component {   state = { value: 0 };

  handleIncrement = () => {   this.setState(prevState => ({value: prevState.value + 1 })); };

  handleDecrement = () => {   this.setState(prevState => ({  value: prevState.value – 1 }));  };

  render() {   return ( <div> {this.state.value}  <button onClick={this.handleIncrement}>+</button>

    <button onClick={this.handleDecrement}>-</button>  </div> )  } }
```

Question: What are hooks?

Hooks are a new feature proposal that lets you use state and other React features without writing a class. Let's see an example of useState hook example,

```jsx
import { useState } from 'react';

function Example() {

  // Declare a new state variable, which we'll call "count"

  const [count, setCount] = useState(0);

  return (   <div>  <p>You clicked {count} times</p>   <button onClick={() => setCount(count + 1)}>
```

Click me   </button> </div>); }

Question: What are the rules needs to follow for hooks?

You need to follow two rules inorder to use hooks

Call Hooks only at the top level of your react functions. i.e, You shouldn't call Hooks inside loops, conditions, or nested functions. This will ensure that Hooks are called in the same order each time a component renders and it preserves the state of Hooks between multiple useState and useEffect calls.

Call Hooks from React Functions only. i.e, You shouldn't call Hooks from regular JavaScript functions.

Question: How to ensure hooks followed the rules in your project?

React team released an ESLint plugin called eslint-plugin-react-hooks that enforces these two rules. You can add this plugin to your project using the below command,

npm install eslint-plugin-react-hooks@next

And apply the below config in your ESLint config file,

// Your ESLint configuration

{ "plugins": [

   // ...

   "react-hooks"],

  "rules": {

   // ...

   "react-hooks/rules-of-hooks": "error" } }

Note: This plugin is intended to use in Create React App by default.

Question: What are the differences between Flux and Redux?

Below are the major differences between Flux and Redux

Flux	Redux
State is mutable	State is immutable
The Store contains both state and change logic	The Store and change logic are separate
There are multiple stores exist	There is only one store exist

All the stores are disconnected and flat   Single store with hierarchical reducers

It has a singleton dispatcher   There is no concept of dispatcher

React components subscribe to the store   Container components uses connect function

Question: What are the benefits of React Router V4?

Below are the main benefits of React Router V4 module,

In React Router v4(version 4), the API is completely about components. A router can be visualized as a single component() which wraps specific child router components().

You don't need to manually set history. The router module will take care history by wrapping routes with component.

The application size is reduced by adding only the specific router module(Web, core, or native)

Can you describe about componentDidCatch lifecycle method signature?

The componentDidCatch lifecycle method is invoked after an error has been thrown by a descendant component. The method receives two parameters,

error: - The error object which was thrown

info: - An object with a componentStack key contains the information about which component threw the error.

The method structure would be as follows

componentDidCatch(error, info)

Question: In which scenarios error boundaries do not catch errors?

Below are the cases in which error boundaries doesn't work

Inside Event handlers

Asynchronous code using setTimeout or requestAnimationFrame callbacks

During Server side rendering

When errors thrown in the error boundary code itself

Question: Why do not you need error boundaries for event handlers?

Error boundaries do not catch errors inside event handlers. Event handlers don't happened or invoked during rendering time unlike render method or lifecycle methods. So React knows how to recover these kind of errors in event handlers. If still you need to catch an error inside event handler, use the regular JavaScript try / catch statement as below

```
class MyComponent extends React.Component {

  constructor(props) {   super(props);   this.state = { error: null };   }

  handleClick = () => {   try {

    // Do something that could throw

  } catch (error) {   this.setState({ error }) } }

  render() {   if (this.state.error) { return <h1>Caught an error.</h1>}

    return <div onClick={this.handleClick}>Click Me</div>  } }
```

The above code is catching the error using vanilla javascript try/catch block instead of error boundaries.

Question: What is the difference between try catch block and error boundaries?

Try catch block works with imperative code whereas error boundaries are meant for declarative code to render on the screen. For example, the try catch block used for below imperative code

```
try { showButton(); } catch (error) {

  // ...

}
```

Whereas error boundaries wrap declarative code as below,

```
<ErrorBoundary> <MyComponent /> </ErrorBoundary>
```

So if an error occurs in a componentDidUpdate method caused by a setState somewhere deep in the tree, it will still correctly propagate to the closest error boundary.

Question: What is the behavior of uncaught errors in react 16?

In React 16, errors that were not caught by any error boundary will result in unmounting of the whole React component tree. The reason behind this decision is that it is worse to leave corrupted UI in place than to completely remove it. For example, it is worse for a payments app to display a wrong amount than to render nothing.

Question:What is the proper placement for error boundaries?

The granularity of error boundaries usage is up to the developer based on project needs. You can follow either of these approaches,

You can wrap top-level route components to display a generic error message for the entire application.

You can also wrap individual components in an error boundary to protect them from crashing the rest of the application.

Question:What is the benefit of component stack trace from error boundary?

Apart from error messages and javascript stack, React16 will display the component stack trace with file names and line numbers using error boundary concept. For example, BuggyCounter component displays the component stack trace as below,

Question:What is the required method to be defined for a class component?

The render() method is the only required method in a class component. i.e, All methods other than render method are optional for a class component.

Question:What are the possible return types of render method?

Below are the list of following types used and return from render method,

React elements: Elements that instruct React to render a DOM node. It includes html elements such as and user defined elements.

Arrays and fragments: Return multiple elements to render as Arrays and Fragments to wrap multiple elements

Portals: Render children into a different DOM subtree.

String and numbers: Render both Strings and Numbers as text nodes in the DOM

Booleans or null: Doesn't render anything but these types are used to conditionally render content.

Question:What is the main purpose of constructor?

The constructor is mainly used for two purposes,

To initialize local state by assigning object to this.state

For binding event handler methods to the instatnce For example, the below code covers both the above casess,

constructor(props) { super(props);

 // Don't call this.setState() here!

this.state = { counter: 0 }; this.handleClick = this.handleClick.bind(this); }

Question:Is it mandatory to define constructor for React component?

No, it is not mandatory. i.e, If you don't initialize state and you don't bind methods, you don't need to implement a constructor for your React component.

Question:What are default props?

The defaultProps are defined as a property on the component class to set the default props for the class. This is used for undefined props, but not for null props. For example, let us create color default prop for the button component,

class MyButton extends React.Component {

 // ...

}

MyButton.defaultProps = {   color: 'red' };

If props.color is not provided then it will set the default value to 'red'. i.e, Whenever you try to access the color prop it uses default value

render() {   return <MyButton /> ; // props.color will be set to red }

Note: If you provide null value then it remains null value.

Question:Why should not call setState in componentWillUnmount?

You should not call setState() in componentWillUnmount() because Once a component instance is unmounted, it will never be mounted again.

Question:What is the purpose of getDerivedStateFromError?

This lifecycle method is invoked after an error has been thrown by a descendant component. It receives the error that was thrown as a parameter and should return a value to update state. The signature of the lifecycle method is as follows,

static getDerivedStateFromError(error)

Let us take error boundary use case with the above lifecycle method for demonistration purpose,

class ErrorBoundary extends React.Component {

 constructor(props) {   super(props);   this.state = { hasError: false }; }

```
static getDerivedStateFromError(error) {

  // Update state so the next render will show the fallback UI.

  return { hasError: true };  }

 render() {    if (this.state.hasError) {

   // You can render any custom fallback UI

   return <h1>Something went wrong.</h1> }

  return this.props.children;  }}
```

Question:What is the methods order when component re-rendered?

An update can be caused by changes to props or state. The below methods are called in the following order when a component is being re-rendered.

static getDerivedStateFromProps()

shouldComponentUpdate()

render()

getSnapshotBeforeUpdate()

componentDidUpdate()

Question:What are the methods invoked during error handling?

Below methods are called when there is an error during rendering, in a lifecycle method, or in the constructor of any child component.

static getDerivedStateFromError()

componentDidCatch()

Question:What is the purpose of displayName class property?

The displayName string is used in debugging messages. Usually, you don't need to set it explicitly because it's inferred from the name of the function or class that defines the component. You might want to set it explicitly if you want to display a different name for debugging purposes or when you create a higher-order component. For example, To ease debugging, choose a display name that communicates that it's the result of a withSubscription HOC.

```
function withSubscription(WrappedComponent) {
```

```
class WithSubscription extends React.Component {/* ... */}

WithSubscription.displayName = `WithSubscription(${getDisplayName(WrappedComponent)})`;

return WithSubscription; }
```

```
function getDisplayName(WrappedComponent) {

return WrappedComponent.displayName || WrappedComponent.name || 'Component';}
```

Question:What is the browser support for react applications?

React supports all popular browsers, including Internet Explorer 9 and above, although some polyfills are required for older browsers such as IE 9 and IE 10. If you use es5-shim and es5-sham polyfill then it even support old browsers that doesn't support ES5 methods.

Question:What is the purpose of unmountComponentAtNode method?

This method is available from react-dom package and it removes a mounted React component from the DOM and clean up its event handlers and state. If no component was mounted in the container, calling this function does nothing. Returns true if a component was unmounted and false if there was no component to unmount. The method signature would be as follows,

```
ReactDOM.unmountComponentAtNode(container)
```

Question:What is code-splitting?

Code-Splitting is a feature supported by bundlers like Webpack and Browserify which can create multiple bundles that can be dynamically loaded at runtime. The react project supports code splitting via dynamic import() feature. For example, in the below code snippets, it will make moduleA.js and all its unique dependencies as a separate chunk that only loads after the user clicks the 'Load' button.
moduleA.js

```
const moduleA = 'Hello';

export { moduleA };
```

App.js

```
import React, { Component } from 'react';

class App extends Component {

handleClick = () => {   import('./moduleA') .then(({ moduleA }) => {

    // Use moduleA
```

```
})    .catch(err => {

  // Handle failure

}); };

 render() {   return (     <div> <button onClick={this.handleClick}>Load</button> </div> ); } }

export default App;
```

Question: What is the benefit of strict mode?

The will be helpful in the below cases

Identifying components with unsafe lifecycle methods.

Warning about legacy string ref API usage.

Detecting unexpected side effects.

Detecting legacy context API.

Warning about deprecated findDOMNode usage

Question: What are Keyed Fragments?

The Fragments declared with the explicit <React.Fragment> syntax may have keys. The general usecase is mapping a collection to an array of fragments as below,

```
function Glossary(props) {   return (   <dl> {props.items.map(item => (

    // Without the `key`, React will fire a key warning

    <React.Fragment key={item.id}>

     <dt>{item.term}</dt>

     <dd>{item.description}</dd>

    </React.Fragment>     ))}

  </dl>   ); }
```

Note: key is the only attribute that can be passed to Fragment. In the future, there might be a support for additional attributes, such as event handlers.

Question: Is it React support all HTML attributes?

As of React 16, both standard or custom DOM attributes are fully supported. Since React components often take both custom and DOM-related props, React uses the camelCase convention just like the DOM APIs. Let us take few props with respect to standard HTML attributes,

<div tabIndex="-1" />   // Just like node.tabIndex DOM API

<div className="Button" /> // Just like node.className DOM API

<input readOnly={true} /> // Just like node.readOnly DOM API

These props work similarly to the corresponding HTML attributes, with the exception of the special cases. It also support all SVG attributes.

Question: What are the limitations with HOCs?

Higher-order components come with a few caveats apart from its benefits. Below are the few listed in an order

Don't Use HOCs Inside the render Method: It is not recommended to apply a HOC to a component within the render method of a component.

```
render() {

  // A new version of EnhancedComponent is created on every render

  // EnhancedComponent1 !== EnhancedComponent2

  const EnhancedComponent = enhance(MyComponent);

  // That causes the entire subtree to unmount/remount each time!

  return <EnhancedComponent />;  }
```

The above code impact performance by remounting a component that causes the state of that component and all of its children to be lost. Instead, apply HOCs outside the component definition so that the resulting component is created only once

Static Methods Must Be Copied Over: When you apply a HOC to a component the new component does not have any of the static methods of the original component

```
// Define a static method

WrappedComponent.staticMethod = function() {/*...*/}

// Now apply a HOC

const EnhancedComponent = enhance(WrappedComponent);
```

// The enhanced component has no static method

typeof EnhancedComponent.staticMethod === 'undefined' // true

You can overcome this by copying the methods onto the container before returning it

```
function enhance(WrappedComponent) {

  class Enhance extends React.Component {/*...*/}

  // Must know exactly which method(s) to copy :(

  Enhance.staticMethod = WrappedComponent.staticMethod;

  return Enhance; }
```

Refs Aren't Passed Through: For HOCs you need to pass through all props to the wrapped component but this does not work for refs. This is because ref is not really a prop similar to key. In this case you need to use the React.forwardRef API

Question: How to debug forwardRefs in DevTools?

React.forwardRef accepts a render function as parameter and DevTools uses this function to determine what to display for the ref forwarding component. For example, If you don't name the render function or not using displayName property then it will appear as "ForwardRef" in the DevTools,

```
const WrappedComponent = React.forwardRef((props, ref) => {

  return <LogProps {...props} forwardedRef={ref} />; });
```

But If you name the render function then it will appear as "ForwardRef(myFunction)"

```
const WrappedComponent = React.forwardRef(

  function myFunction(props, ref) {    return <LogProps {...props} forwardedRef={ref} />;  });
```

As an alternative, You can also set displayName property for forwardRef function,

```
function logProps(Component) {  class LogProps extends React.Component {

    // ...

  }

  function forwardRef(props, ref) {    return <LogProps {...props} forwardedRef={ref} />; }

  // Give this component a more helpful display name in DevTools.
```

```
// e.g. "ForwardRef(logProps(MyComponent))"

const name = Component.displayName || Component.name;

forwardRef.displayName = `logProps(${name})`;

return React.forwardRef(forwardRef); }
```

Question: When component props defaults to true?

If you pass no value for a prop, it defaults to true. This behavior is available so that it matches the behavior of HTML. For example, below expressions are equivalent,

```
<MyInput autocomplete />

<MyInput autocomplete={true} />
```

Note: It is not recommend using this approach because it can be confused with the ES6 object shorthand (example, {name} which is short for {name: name})

Question: What is NextJS and major features of it?

Next.js is a popular and lightweight framework for static and server-rendered applications built with React. It also provides styling and routing solutions. Below are the major features provided by NextJS,

Server-rendered by default

Automatic code splitting for faster page loads

Simple client-side routing (page based)

Webpack-based dev environment which supports (HMR)

Able to implement with Express or any other Node.js HTTP server

Customizable with your own Babel and Webpack configurations

Question: How do you pass an event handler to a component?

You can pass event handlers and other functions as props to child components. It can be used in child component as below,

```
<button onClick={this.handleClick}>
```

Question: Is it good to use arrow functions in render methods?

Yes, You can use. It is often the easiest way to pass parameters to callback functions. But you need to optimize the performance while using it.

```jsx
class Foo extends Component {

  handleClick() {   console.log('Click happened'); }

  render() {   return <button onClick={() => this.handleClick()}>Click Me</button>; } }
```

Note: Using an arrow function in render method creates a new function each time the component renders, which may have performance implications

Question: How to prevent a function from being called multiple times?

If you use an event handler such as onClick or onScroll and want to prevent the callback from being fired too quickly, then you can limit the rate at which callback is executed. This can be achieved in the below possible ways,

Throttling: Changes based on a time based frequency. For example, it can be used using _.throttle lodash function

Debouncing: Publish changes after a period of inactivity. For example, it can be used using _.debounce lodash function

RequestAnimationFrame throttling: Changes based on requestAnimationFrame. For example, it can be used using raf-schd lodash function

Question: How JSX prevents Injection Attacks?

React DOM escapes any values embedded in JSX before rendering them. Thus it ensures that you can never inject anything that's not explicitly written in your application. Everything is converted to a string before being rendered. For example, you can embed user input as below,

```jsx
const name = response.potentiallyMaliciousInput;
```

```jsx
const element = <h1>{name}</h1>;
```

This way you can prevent XSS(Cross-site-scripting) attacks in the application.

Question: How do you update rendered elements?

You can update UI(represented by rendered element) by passing the newly created element to ReactDOM's render method. For example, lets take a ticking clock example, where it updates the time by calling render method multiple times,

```jsx
function tick() {   const element = ( <div>
```

```jsx
  <h1>Hello, world!</h1>   <h2>It is {new Date().toLocaleTimeString()}.</h2></div> );
```

```jsx
ReactDOM.render(element, document.getElementById('root')); }
```

setInterval(tick, 1000);

Question: How do you say that props are read only?

When you declare a component as a function or a class, it must never modify its own props. Let us take a below capital function,

function capital(amount, interest) {   return amount + interest; }

The above function is called "pure" because it does not attempt to change their inputs, and always return the same result for the same inputs. Hence, React has a single rule saying "All React components must act like pure functions with respect to their props."

Question: How do you say that state updates are merged?

When you call setState() in the component, React merges the object you provide into the current state. For example, let us take a facebook user with posts and comments details as state variables,

  constructor(props) {   super(props);

   this.state = {   posts: [], comments: [] }; }

Now you can update them independently with separate setState() calls as below,

  componentDidMount() {

    fetchPosts().then(response => {   this.setState({   posts: response.posts   }); });

    fetchComments().then(response => { this.setState({ comments: response.comments }); }); }

As mentioned in the above code snippets, this.setState({comments}) updates only comments variable without modifying or replacing posts variable.

Question: How do you pass arguments to an event handler?

During iterations or loops, it is common to pass an extra parameter to an event handler. This can be achieved through arrow functions or bind method. Let us take an example of user details updated in a grid,

<button onClick={(e) => this.updateUser(userId, e)}>Update User details</button>

<button onClick={this.updateUser.bind(this, userId)}>Update User details</button>

In both the approaches, the synthetic argument e is passed as a second argument. You need to pass it explicitly for arrow functions and it forwarded automatically for bind method.

Question: How to prevent component from rendering?

You can prevent component from rendering by returning null based on specific condition. This way it can conditionally render component.

```
function Greeting(props) { if (!props.loggedIn) {   return null;  }

 return (   <div className="greeting"> welcome, {props.name}   </div> ); }

class User extends React.Component {

 constructor(props) { super(props);   this.state = {loggedIn: false, name: 'John'}; }

 render() {   return (<div>

    //Prevent component render if it is not loggedIn

    <Greeting loggedIn={this.state.loggedIn} /> <UserDetails name={this.state.name}> </div> );  }
```

In the above example, the greeting component skips its rendering section by applying condition and returning null value.

Question: What are the conditions to safely use the index as a key?

There are three conditions to make sure, it is safe use the index as a key.

The list and items are static– they are not computed and do not change

The items in the list have no ids

The list is never reordered or filtered.

Question: IS it keys should be globally unique?

Keys used within arrays should be unique among their siblings but they don't need to be globally unique. i.e, You can use the same keys withtwo different arrays. For example, the below book component uses two arrays with different arrays,

```
function Book(props) { const index = (   <ul>  {props.pages.map((page) =>

    <li key={page.id}>    {page.title}   </li>    )}   </ul> )

 const content = props.pages.map((page) =>

  <div key={page.id}>    <h3>{page.title}</h3>    <p>{page.content}</p>
<p>{page.pageNumber}</p>   </div> );

 return (   <div>   {index}   <hr />   {content}   </div> );}
```

Question: What is the popular choice for form handling?

Formik is a form library for react which provides solutions such as validation, keeping track of the visited fields, and handling form submission. In detail, You can categorize them as follows,

Getting values in and out of form state

Validation and error messages

Handling form submission

It is used to create a scalable, performant, form helper with a minimal API to solve annoying stuff.

Question: What are the advantages of formic over redux form library?

Below are the main reasons to recommend formik over redux form library

The form state is inherently short-term and local, so tracking it in Redux (or any kind of Flux library) is unnecessary.

Redux-Form calls your entire top-level Redux reducer multiple times ON EVERY SINGLE KEYSTROKE. This way it increases input latency for large apps.

Redux-Form is 22.5 kB minified gzipped whereas Formik is 12.7 kB

Question: Why do you not required to use inheritance?

In React, it is recommend using composition instead of inheritance to reuse code between components. Both Props and composition give you all the flexibility you need to customize a component's look and behavior in an explicit and safe way. Whereas, If you want to reuse non-UI functionality between components, it is suggested to extracting it into a separate JavaScript module. Later components import it and use that function, object, or a class, without extending it.

Question: Can I use web components in react application?

Yes, you can use web components in a react application. Even though many developers won't use this combination, it may require especially if you are using third-party UI components that are written using Web Components. For example, let us use Vaadin date picker web component as below,

import React, { Component } from 'react';

import './App.css';

import '@vaadin/vaadin-date-picker';

```
class App extends Component {

  render() {   return ( <div className="App"> <vaadin-date-picker label="When were you
born?"></vaadin-date-picker>      </div>); } }

export default App;
```

Question: What is dynamic import?

The dynamic import() syntax is a ECMAScript proposal not currently part of the language standard. It is expected to be accepted in the near future. You can achieve code-splitting into your app using dynamic import(). Let's take an example of addition,

Normal Import

```
import { add } from './math';

console.log(add(10, 20));
```

Dynamic Import

```
import("./math").then(math => { console.log(math.add(10, 20)); });
```

Question: What are loadable components?

If you want to do code-splitting in a server rendered app, it is recommend to use Loadable Components because React.lazy and Suspense is not yet available for server-side rendering. Loadable lets you render a dynamic import as a regular component. Lets take an example,

```
import loadable from '@loadable/component'

const OtherComponent = loadable(() => import('./OtherComponent'))

function MyComponent() {  return (

   <div>     <OtherComponent /> </div> ) }
```

Now OtherComponent will be loaded in a separated bundle

Question: What is suspense component?

If the module containing the dynamic import is not yet loaded by the time parent component renders, you must show some fallback content while you're waiting for it to load using a loading indicator. This can be done using Suspense component. For example, the below code uses suspense component,

```
const OtherComponent = React.lazy(() => import('./OtherComponent'));
```

function MyComponent() { return (<div> <Suspense fallback={<div>Loading...</div>}>

<OtherComponent />   </Suspense> </div>); }

As mentioned in the above code, Suspense is wrapped above the lazy component.

Question: What is route based code splitting?

One of the best place to do code splitting is with routes. The entire page is going to re-render at once so users are unlikely to interact with other elements in the page at the same time. Due to this, the user experience won't be disturbed. Let us take an example of route based website using libraries like React Router with React.lazy,

```
import { BrowserRouter as Router, Route, Switch } from 'react-router-dom';

import React, { Suspense, lazy } from 'react';

const Home = lazy(() => import('./routes/Home'));

const About = lazy(() => import('./routes/About'));

const App = () => (  <Router>    <Suspense fallback={<div>Loading...</div>}>

    <Switch>      <Route exact path="/" component={Home}/>

 <Route path="/about" component={About}/>    </Switch> </Suspense></Router> );
```

In the above code, the code splitting will happen at each route level.

Question: Give an example on How to use context?

Context is designed to share data that can be considered global for a tree of React components. For example, in the code below lets manually thread through a "theme" prop in order to style the Button component.

```
//Lets create a context with a default theme value "luna"

const ThemeContext = React.createContext('luna');

// Create App component where it uses provider to pass theme value in the tree

class App extends React.Component {

render() {   return (  <ThemeContext.Provider value="nova"> <Toolbar /> </ThemeContext.Provider>
); } }

// A middle component where you don't need to pass theme prop anymore
```

```jsx
function Toolbar(props) {  return (   <div>    <ThemedButton />   </div> );}
```

// Lets read theme value in the button component to use

```jsx
class ThemedButton extends React.Component {

  static contextType = ThemeContext;

  render() {   return <Button theme={this.context} />;  }}
```

Question: What is the purpose of default value in context?

The defaultValue argument is only used when a component does not have a matching Provider above it in the tree. This can be helpful for testing components in isolation without wrapping them. Below code snippet provides default theme value as Luna.

```jsx
const MyContext = React.createContext(defaultValue);
```

Question: How do you use contextType?

ContextType is used to consume the context object. The contextType property can be used in two ways,

contextType as property of class: The contextType property on a class can be assigned a Context object created by React.createContext(). After that, you can consume the nearest current value of that Context type using this.context in any of the lifecycle methods and render function. Lets assign contextType property on MyClass as below,

```jsx
class MyClass extends React.Component {  componentDidMount() {

  let value = this.context;

   /* perform a side-effect at mount using the value of MyContext */

  }

  componentDidUpdate() {   let value = this.context;

   /* ... */

  }

  componentWillUnmount() {   let value = this.context;

   /* ... */

  }
```

```
render() {    let value = this.context;

  /* render something based on the value of MyContext */

}}
```

```
MyClass.contextType = MyContext;
```

Static field You can use a static class field to initialize your contextType using public class field syntax.

```
class MyClass extends React.Component {  static contextType = MyContext;

  render() {    let value = this.context;

  /* render something based on the value */

}}
```

Question: What is a consumer?

A Consumer is a React component that subscribes to context changes. It requires a function as a child which receives current context value as argument and returns a react node. The value argument passed to the function will be equal to the value prop of the closest Provider for this context above in the tree. Lets take a simple example,

```
<MyContext.Consumer>  {value => /* render something based on the context value */}

</MyContext.Consumer>
```

Question: How do you solve performance corner cases while using context?

The context uses reference identity to determine when to re-render, there are some gotchas that could trigger unintentional renders in consumers when a provider's parent re-renders. For example, the code below will re-render all consumers every time the Provider re-renders because a new object is always created for value.

```
class App extends React.Component {

  render() {    return ( <Provider value={{something: 'something'}}>  <Toolbar /> </Provider> ); }}
```

This can be solved by lifting up the value to parent state,

```
class App extends React.Component {

  constructor(props) {    super(props);

    this.state = {     value: {something: 'something'},};}
```

```jsx
render() {

  return (    <Provider value={this.state.value}> <Toolbar />   </Provider> ); } }
```

Question: What is the purpose of forward ref in HOCs?

Refs will not get passed through because ref is not a prop. It handled differently by React just like key. If you add a ref to a HOC, the ref will refer to the outermost container component, not the wrapped component. In this case, you can use Forward Ref API. For example, we can explicitly forward refs to the inner FancyButton component using the React.forwardRef API. The below HOC logs all props,

```jsx
function logProps(Component) {

  class LogProps extends React.Component {   componentDidUpdate(prevProps) {

    console.log('old props:', prevProps);     console.log('new props:', this.props); }

   render() {    const {forwardedRef, ...rest} = this.props;

    // Assign the custom prop "forwardedRef" as a ref

    return <Component ref={forwardedRef} {...rest} />;   } }

  return React.forwardRef((props, ref) => { return <LogProps {...props} forwardedRef={ref} />; }); }
```

Let's use this HOC to log all props that get passed to our "fancy button" component,

```jsx
class FancyButton extends React.Component {

  focus() {

   // ...

  }

  // ...

}

export default logProps(FancyButton);
```

Now lets create a ref and pass it to FancyButton component. In this case, you can set focus to button element.

```jsx
import FancyButton from './FancyButton';

const ref = React.createRef();

ref.current.focus();
```

```jsx
<FancyButton  label="Click Me" handleClick={handleClick}  ref={ref} />;
```

Question: Is it ref argument available for all functions or class components?

Regular function or class components don't receive the ref argument, and ref is not available in props either. The second ref argument only exists when you define a component with React.forwardRef call.

Question: Why do you need additional care for component libraries while using forward refs?

When you start using forwardRef in a component library, you should treat it as a breaking change and release a new major version of your library. This is because your library likely has a different behavior such as what refs get assigned to, and what types are exported. These changes can break apps and other libraries that depend on the old behavior.

Question: How to create react class components without ES6?

If you don't use ES6 then you may need to use the create-react-class module instead. For default props, you need to define getDefaultProps() as a function on the passed object. Whereas for initial state, you have to provide a separate getInitialState method that returns the initial state.

```jsx
var Greeting = createReactClass({  getDefaultProps: function() {

    return {     name: 'Jhohn' }; },

  getInitialState: function() {    return {message: this.props.message};  },

  handleClick: function() {    console.log(this.state.message); },

  render: function() {   return <h1>Hello, {this.props.name}</h1>; }});
```

Note: If you use createReactClass then autobinding is available for all methods. i.e, You don't need to use .bind(this) with in constructor for event handlers.

Question: Is it possible to use react without JSX?

Yes, JSX is not mandatory for using React. Actually it is convenient when you don't want to set up compilation in your build environment. Each JSX element is just syntactic sugar for calling React.createElement(component, props, ...children). For example, let us take a greeting example with JSX,

```jsx
class Greeting extends React.Component {  render() {

  return <div>Hello {this.props.message}</div>;  }}

ReactDOM.render(  <Greeting message="World" />,

  document.getElementById('root'));
```

You can write the same code without JSX as below,

```
class Greeting extends React.Component {

  render() {   return React.createElement('div', null, `Hello ${this.props.message}`);  }}

ReactDOM.render(  React.createElement(Greeting, {message: 'World'}, null),

  document.getElementById('root'));
```

Question: What is diffing algorithm?

React needs to use algorithms to find out how to efficiently update the UI to match the most recent tree. The diffing algorithms is generating the minimum number of operations to transform one tree into another. However, the algorithms have a complexity in the order of O(n3) where n is the number of elements in the tree. In this case, for displaying 1000 elements would require in the order of one billion comparisons. This is far too expensive. Instead, React implements a heuristic O(n) algorithm based on two assumptions:

Two elements of different types will produce different trees.

The developer can hint at which child elements may be stable across different renders with a key prop.

Question: What are the rules covered by diffing algorithm?

When diffing two trees, React first compares the two root elements. The behavior is different depending on the types of the root elements. It covers the below rules during reconsilation algorithm,

Elements Of Different Types: Whenever the root elements have different types, React will tear down the old tree and build the new tree from scratch. For example, elements to , or from to of different types lead a full rebuild.

DOM Elements Of The Same Type: When comparing two React DOM elements of the same type, React looks at the attributes of both, keeps the same underlying DOM node, and only updates the changed attributes. Lets take an example with same DOM eleemnts except className attribute,

<div className="show" title="ReactJS" />

<div className="hide" title="ReactJS" />

Component Elements Of The Same Type: When a component updates, the instance stays the same, so that state is maintained across renders. React updates the props of the underlying component instance to match the new element, and calls componentWillReceiveProps() and componentWillUpdate() on the underlying instance. After that, the render() method is called and the diff algorithm recurses on the previous result and the new result.

Recursing On Children: when recursing on the children of a DOM node, React just iterates over both lists of children at the same time and generates a mutation whenever there's a difference. For example, when adding an element at the end of the children, converting between these two trees works well.

```
<ul> <li>first</li><li>second</li></ul><ul> <li>first</li>  <li>second</li> <li>third</li></ul>
```

Handling keys: React supports a key attribute. When children have keys, React uses the key to match children in the original tree with children in the subsequent tree. For example, adding a key can make the tree conversion efficient,

```
<ul> <li key="2015">Duke</li> <li key="2016">Villanova</li></ul>

<ul>

  <li key="2014">Connecticut</li>

  <li key="2015">Duke</li>

  <li key="2016">Villanova</li>

</ul>
```

Question: when do you need to use refs?

There are few use cases to go for refs

Managing focus, text selection, or media playback.

Triggering imperative animations.

Integrating with third-party DOM libraries.

Question: Is it prop must be named as render for render props?

Even though the pattern named render props, you don't have to use a prop named render to use this pattern. i.e, Any prop that is a function that a component uses to know what to render is technically a "render prop". Lets take an example with the children prop for render props,

```
<Mouse children={mouse => ( <p>The mouse position is {mouse.x}, {mouse.y}</p>)}/>
```

Actually children prop doesn't need to be named in the list of "attributes" in JSX element. Instead, you can keep it directly inside element,

```
<Mouse>  {mouse => (   <p>The mouse position is {mouse.x}, {mouse.y}</p>)} </Mouse>
```

While using this above technique(without any name), explicitly state that children should be a function in your propTypes.

```
Mouse.propTypes = {  children: PropTypes.func.isRequired  };
```

Question: What are the problems of using render props with pure components?

If you create a function inside a render method, it negates the purpose of pure component. Because the shallow prop comparison will always return false for new props, and each render in this case will generate a new value for the render prop. You can solve this issue by defining the render function as instance method.

Question: How do you create HOC using render props?

You can implement most higher-order components (HOC) using a regular component with a render prop. For example, if you would prefer to have a withMouse HOC instead of a component, you could easily create one using a regular with a render prop.

```
function withMouse(Component) {  return class extends React.Component {

  render() {     return (  <Mouse render={mouse => (

      <Component {...this.props} mouse={mouse} />     )}/>     );  } }}
```

This way render props gives the flexibility of using either pattern.

Question: What is windowing technique?

Windowing is a technique that only renders a small subset of your rows at any given time, and can dramatically reduce the time it takes to re-render the components as well as the number of DOM nodes created. If your application renders long lists of data then this technique is recommended. Both react-window and react-virtualized are popular windowing libraries which provides several reusable components for displaying lists, grids, and tabular data.

Question: How do you print falsy values in JSX?

The falsy values such as false, null, undefined, and true are valid children but they don't render anything. If you still want to display them then you need to convert it to string. Let's take an example on how to convert to a string,

```
<div>  My JavaScript variable is {String(myVariable)}.</div>
```

Question: What is the typical use case of portals?

React portals are very useful when a parent component has overflow: hidden or has properties that affect the stacking context(z-index,position,opacity etc styles) and you need to visually "break out" of its container. For example, dialogs, global message notifications, hovercards, and tooltips.

Question: How do you set default value for uncontrolled component?

In React, the value attribute on form elements will override the value in the DOM. With an uncontrolled component, you might want React to specify the initial value, but leave subsequent updates uncontrolled. To handle this case, you can specify a defaultValue attribute instead of value.

```
render() { return ( <form onSubmit={this.handleSubmit}>

  <label> User Name: <input defaultValue="John" type="text" ref={this.input} /> </label>

    <input type="submit" value="Submit" /> </form> );}
```

The same applies for select and textArea inputs. But you need to use defaultChecked for checkbox and radio inputs.

Question: What is your favorite React stack?

Even though the tech stack varies from developer to developer, the most popular stack is used in react boilerplate project code. It mainly uses Redux and redux-saga for state management and asynchronous side-effects, react-router for routing purpose, styled-components for styling react components, axios for invoking REST api, and other supported stack such as webpack, reselect, ESNext, Babel. You can clone the project https://github.com/react-boilerplate/react-boilerplate and start working on any new react project.

Question: What is the difference between Real DOM and Virtual DOM?

Below are the main differences between Real DOM and Virtual DOM,

Real DOM	Virtual DOM
Updates are slow	Updates are fast
DOM manipulation is very expensive.	DOM manipulation is very easy
You can update HTML directly.	You Can't directly update HTML
It causes too much of memory wastage	There is no memory wastage
Creates a new DOM if element updates	It updates the JSX if element update

Question: How to add a bootstrap for a react application?

Bootstrap can be added to your React app in a three possible ways

Using the Bootstrap CDN: This is the easiest way to add bootstrap. Add both bootstrap CSS and JS resources in a head tag.

Bootstrap as Dependency: If you are using a build tool or a module bundler such as Webpack, then this is the preferred option for adding Bootstrap to your React application

npm install bootstrap

``

React Bootstrap Package: In this case, you can add Bootstrap to our React app is by using a package that has rebuilt Bootstrap components to work particularly as React components. Below packages are popular in this category,

react-bootstrap

reactstrap

Question: Can you list down top websites or applications using react as front end framework?

Below are the top 10 websites using React as their front-end framework,

Facebook

Uber

Instagram

WhatsApp

Khan Academy

Airbnb

Dropbox

Flipboard

Netflix

PayPal